CHÛSHINGURA

AN EXPOSITION

BY

SAKAE SHIOYA, Ph. M. (Chicago)

Author of 'When I was a Boy in Japan'
Translator of 'Namiko'
and 'The Pagoda'

Illustrated with Hiroshige's Coloured Plates

(SECOND EDITION)

TOKYO

THE HOKUSEIDO PRESS

PRINTED IN JAPAN

Introductory Note to the Second Edition

Owing to the general damage suffered in the Pacific War, the original edition of the book was destroyed, paper mould and all, at the publishers and much to the disappointment of those who wish to read it, was long left out of print. But happy to say, the Hokuseido Press have recently reprinted it and it is now offered to the public, carefully revised.

THE AUTHOR

Tokyo, October, 1956

PREFACE

Considering the great importance attached to the play *Chûshingura* and the historical fact on which it was founded, the vendetta of the Akô retainers, as indispensable material to students of Japanese thought and spirit, old and yet still surviving in part, it is surprising to find that only a few English books on them have appeared and those quite incomplete or misleading for the right understanding of the subject. Of the *Chûshingura* two translations of the text have been published : one by Frederick Victor Dickins in 1875 and the other by Jûkichi Inouye in 1910. The former is told in story form with the divisions of the acts retained, and though the more readable of the two, it has no comments or explanatory introduction to it except a brief translator's note. The latter is a direct translation of the text and is very convenient for getting a correct idea of the original. It has a lengthy introduction, too, giving accounts of the Akô vendetta, social conditions in the Tokugawa period, the characteristics of *bushido*, and the bearing of the historical facts on the *Chûshingura*. In fact this forms a handy help to the comprehension of the play ; still it cannot escape from the charge of being rather cursory, and in common with all the English versions of the Akô story, it misses some cardinal points, while it leaves entirely out of account such results as have been attained by recent researches of the play.

As to the English versions of the story, Mitford's *Forty-seven Ronin* in the *Tales of Old Japan* (1871) is still, rather curiously, taken as true by Western readers. It is anyway too short for a full account of the story and besides containing some mistakes in names and incidents, it fails to give some of the vital points.   And this also can be said, more or less, of the other versions in English, long or short.   This resulted from the facts that the writers took the story merely from what they had heard, not caring about the authenticity of it or rather believing that it was authentic enough to be recounted as it was.

There was time in the Meiji era when the Akô story formed the most popular theme for story-tellers and romance writers, who, aiming to arouse interest in their audience or readers, did not hesitate to introduce fictitious matters or to slur over some important parts just to suit their fancy. And so, though the same in the main, the story as generally known has come to be a jumble of all these, and an English rendering of it done indiscriminately has to suffer accordingly.

Of course, in the meanwhile, historical researches have been conducted by scholars to get the true facts of the case. And now we have at least one book which may be considered really reliable, entitled *Genroku-Kwaikyo-Roku* (*A Record of the Stirring Enterprise of the Genroku Era*) by Fukumoto-Nichinan.   Everything being clearly explained in it, the book has come to be a most valuable help for studying the story.   But as it was published as late as 1909, it has not as yet had sufficient time to eliminate all the errors crusted about the story in people's minds.   So it is now high time to recount the story with this as our basis, and it is done so in this book for the first time in English.

The story on which the *Chûshingura* was founded being thus authenticated, the relation between the two will be

seen in a new light.   What is wanting in the play will be
readily and fully supplied, while the merits the play possesses in spite of its divergence from the actual story will
be taken at their true value.   And it is hoped that this new
attempt at elucidation will be of real help to a correct
appreciation of the play.

THE AUTHOR.

Tokyo, December, 1939.

Contents

PAGE

Introductory Note to the Second Edition . . v

Preface vii

CHAPTER

I. A General Survey 1

II. The Loyal Retainers of Akô—I 9

    The Death of Asano, Lord of Akô 9

    The Surrender of the Akô Castle 18

III. The Loyal Retainers of Akô—II 43

    Ôishi at Yamashina 43

    Retribution at Last ! 66

IV. The Spirit of the Samurai 82

    Following One's Lord in Death 83

    The Code of Vengeance 91

    The Civil Duty of the Samurai 98

    The Custom of *Seppuku* 105

    The Influence of the Samurai Spirit 107

V. The *Chûshingura*—I 115

    Act I. At Tsurugaoka Hachiman 115

    Act II. The Anger of Wakasanosuke . . 119

    Act III. The Quarrel of Enya with Moronao 123

    Act IV. The Death of Enya 134

    Act V. The Night Adventure of Kampei . 143

    Act VI. The Death of Kampei 151

VI. The *Chûshingura*—II 163

    Act VII. Yuranosuke Leads a Dissolute Life 163

    Act VIII. The Bridal Journey 181

ACT IX. THE REPENTANCE OF HONZÔ . . . 184

ACT X. THE MANLINESS OF GIHEI 200

ACT XI. RETRIBUTION 216

VII. APPRECIATION 225

INDEX 231

COLOURED PLATES

After HIROSHIGE (1797–1858)

PLATE   I.   For the Finale   . . . . *Frontispiece*

FACING PAGE

PLATE   II.   For Act I   114

PLATE III.   For Act IV ʳ34

PLATE IV.   For Act VIII   182

CHAPTER I

A GENERAL SURVEY

The *Chûshingura* is the most famous of all the old Japanese plays. It is so because it was based on that famous incident in history known as the Akô vendetta, unanimously considered in Japan to be an unparalleled example of the display of the true samurai spirit, and also because, restricted as it was in its dramatization, it has come to be recognized as the representative play on the subject among many attempts of the kind.

The story of the play and the historical facts on which it was founded will be given in detail later on, but as it will be convenient to some readers to get at the start some rough information about both play and facts, which are found to be the same at bottom, just the gist of it is given here to begin with. A certain lord in feudal times, Lord Asano of Akô in history and Lord Enya in the play, was so much enraged by insults offered him by the officer appointed to advise him on some points of ceremony that he essayed to kill him when both were on duty in the palace. His attempt failed, but because of his grievous offence, he was sentenced to capital punishment, this involving the confiscation of his fief and the extermination of his house, while his enemy was adjudged innocent and acquitted. His retainers, numbering some three hundred, were now left masterless and without pay, but were free to go where they would to get their living; yet some of them could not feel that they were absolved from their duty to their dead lord, and, impelled by the samurai spirit, they, forty-seven in number, banded themselves together and resolved to avenge their master's wrongs upon his enemy. And this they finally effected after nearly two years of suffering and untiring efforts, and gladly met their doom.

Now the *Chûshingura* is a dramatization of this story, made in 1748 by Takeda-Izumo in collaboration with two others, its full title being *Kanadehon-Chûshingura (Forty-seven Exemplary Loyal Subjects)*. The story of the loyal subjects being so great in popular appeal, since the occurrence of the historical event in 1702 more than a hundred plays were attempted on the subject from time to time, but none succeeded so well as the *Chûshingura* because of its undoubted excellence in working out the material.

The term *chûshingura* belongs especially to this play, but as it is a happy expression for ' a number of faithful subjects' particularly in reference to the loyal Akô retainers, it is often made use of, with some casual qualifications, for the titles of various novels or stories of the historical incidents, as if the historical facts and their stage version were practically one and the same in almost every respect. Indeed, they are so in spirit and plot in general, ending in the same issue, but in the outward garb of setting, names of characters, initial incidents, and some accessory matters, the play is quite different from the historical facts. How this happened to be so may be understood from the policy followed by the Tokugawa Government then in power.

That Government prohibited on principle the dramatization of contemporary events just as they were, using the real names of persons in authority at the time, simply to protect them from any scandals which might arise in consequence. So the first play on the subject, which appeared less than two weeks after the Akô affair was finally disposed of, in the second month of 1703 (by the old calendar), treated it as another form of the famous vendetta of the Soga brothers which had occurred half a century earlier. But as the latter event was too well known and too close to the minds of the people to admit of any alteration, the attempt was only short-lived, and no others ever succeeded till we come to a play entitled *Goban-Taiheiki* by Chikamatsu-Monzayemon, the Shakespeare of Japan, first put on the stage in 1706. There was no reason why a work by the great dramatist should fail, and this play held the boards for a long time, an adaptation of it being played even as late as the middle of the Meiji era by Nakamura-Ganjirô, the unsurpassed actor of Chikamatsu drama. It is a pity, however, that the play was too short to be comprehensive, being merely a sequel to another play called *Kenkôhôshi-Monomiguruma*, which treated of some of the opening incidents, and consisting of only one act, which contained two scenes from the incidents towards the end of the story. But this play with the preceding one did admirable service in suggesting proper settings and some of the historical characters to enact the parts of real persons in the story, which suggestions were welcomed and closely followed by nearly all the later playwrights of the Tokugawa period, who tried their hands at its dramatization.

There the whole scene was carried back to the time covered in that famous historical story-book, the *Taiheiki*, that is, to the time of the first Shogun Takauji of the Ashikaga line in the middle of the fifteeth century, and the historical events concerning Kira-Kôzukenosuke and Asano-Takuminokami which led to the great vendetta were replaced by the equally fatal quarrel—though of a different sort—between Kôno-Moronao and Enya-Hangwan, noted warriors figuring in the *Taiheiki*, which gave rise to a similar catastrophe with the great leader and hero Ôishi-Kurano-suke under the name of Ôboshi-Yuranosuke. It fills us with regret to think that with such an ingenious ground-work as this, Chikamatsu missed dramatizing the event in full; but for this the time did not seem as yet to be ripe, and though he was keen enough to see the chance, he failed to do it more than partial justice. Some forty years more elapsed, during which many plays of more or less merit and more complete than Chikamatsu's appeared, vying for popular favour; but it needed the efforts of some unusually talented actor to bring the subject close to the hearts of the people and arouse their unbounded enthusiasm, and thus give an impetus to the production of a really excellent play.

It was in 1746 and 7 that a noted actor of the time, Sawamura-Sôjûrô, made a great hit in Osaka and Kyoto, playing the part of Yamagishi-Kunai (another stage-name for Ôishi-Kuranosuke). The play he acted in does not concern us very much, for it was certainly his acting and not the play that moved the audience. Takeda-Izumo, the famous writer of puppet-plays, noted the actor's success, and in default of a good play, with his skill in plot-construction and stage technique, at once set about to produce in col-laboration with two others the *Chûshingura* in the following year, as we have already mentioned.

What the play is will be described in detail in separate chapters, but following the groundwork supplied by Chi-kamatsu, the writers took in as much of the historical facts as enabled them to develop a story, enriching it with romantic variations, and the work resulted as we see in such a well-knit, artistic piece as to have a life of its own, quite independent of the history itself. Its merit was at once recognized, and it became before long the most celebrated version of the vendetta and practically drove all the other plays of the same nature off the stage.

The play is a long one, having eleven acts in all. And it may be wondered how a play almost three times as long as an ordinary present-day drama could be put on the boards all at one time. Indeed, they are compelled now-adays to give only selections from it at a theatre, but in the Tokugawa period, when the play was produced, the theatre used to open at about eight in the morning and the performances lasted far into the evening, so that there was no difficulty in going all through in one day. How happy were the days when play-going could be indulged in so long at a stretch, so that the pleasant impressions left by it would be sure to pass into one's dreams, even ting-ing with a visionary haze the daylight of reality to which one awoke! Be that as it may, it was entirely due to this custom that we have to-day such a classical play of the Akô retainers in which their deeds are interestingly treated in full in memory of their noble spirit.

The *Chûshingura* on the stage may, of course, be enjoyed in several ways according to the extent of one's acquaintance with the play. But apart from the artistic appreciation of acting in the form peculiar to Japanese classical play , of which only dramatic experts are really capable, anybody can feast his eyes on the splendour of costumes and the beauty of scenes of the feudal days, which being idealized to modern eyes because of the distance in time, we may rejoice in as lovely pieces out of the past brought to life again for the nonce, and which to Westerners may suggest big *genre* pictures by some old master superbly coloured, allowing peeps into the real world of Old Japan. This is certainly delightful either way, and must be the first impression one gets from the performance; such is, however, true not only of the *Chûshingura* but of any other of the fine classical plays known as *kabuki*, and if one does not go much further than this and merely follows the story, here diverted at some peculiar manners and there puzzled over the working of apparently queer psychology, one will come away not much the wiser.

Now even among those who look a little deeper into the play, we find this difference in their way of facing it according as the spectator is a Japanese or a Western visitor without any foreknowledge of what the play is: that while the latter will see the play and try to deduce everything only from what has struck his eyes, the former will also see and enjoy the play, but at the same time review in mind the historical facts at the back of it, taking distorted points at their true value, supplying from history what is lacking, and differentiating what is essential from what is not. For the play is a play, a piece of art, made primarily to give delight and not to be an authentic record of history, and so we need the discriminating eye in order not to be misled by the glamour of the deft weaving of the plot in places where it is only aiming to entertain and hold the spectator's interest. You will thus have to be told which is the proper way to approach the play, the way you must take even to come to something like a true understanding of what is treasured in that much-valued stuff.

For this it is quite necessary to be equipped at the outset with a reasonable amount of information concerning the real facts of the subject of the play, much more, of course, than has been given already, and to comprehend clearly the motive, too, that led the Akô retainers to that desperate effort as well as some phases of life peculiar to the samurai class ; to help grasp all which points some of the following chapters will be devoted. But before going into them, it will be well to glance over the way the real story has been received by the Japanese in order to understand the feeling with which they sit down to the play.

A good book or two on the subject appeared later in the Tokugawa period, but it was in the Meiji era, when people were free to discuss the doings of the men concerned, that histories and novels on it flooded the market in response to the rising demand, while various renderings by noted story-tellers and moving recitatives in what is known as *naniwa-bushi* drew crowds of eager people to the music halls. And though they allowed themselves room for the play of fancy, so that fictitious matters crept in here and there, and it needed the effort of such a historian as Fukumoto-Nichinan (1857–1921) to sweep the dust off this precious human document and burnish it to bring out its old imperishable lustre in his *Genroku-Kwaikyo-Roku (A Record of the Stirring Enterprise in the Genroku Era)*, which appeared in 1909, on the whole they did much to impress us with the fact that the Akô event was not a mere historical happening but an actual drama flowering out of the feudal society in its most cultured state, the drama which is an artistic embodiment of *bushidô* or the spirit of the samurai in its purest form, fostered and tempered in the troublous days of old and handed down to us as a living flame which makes a Japanese what he should be. Thus it is always with reverence that we touch the heart of the story, and at the same time we read or listen to its recounting with a gratifying sense of elation, the like of which Western men in olden days must have experienced in listening to minstrels thrumming and reciting their favourite heroic tales. And this is also the case in part w.th us in sitting before a performance of the *Chûshingura*, got up as it is,—a state of mind into which it will be well for Westerners to try to enter.

CHAPTER II

THE LOYAL RETAINERS OF AKÔ—I

THE DEATH OF ASANO, LORD OF AKÔ

It was an established custom under the Tokugawa rule (1603–1868) for the Shogun to present annually to the Imperial Court in Kyoto a large sum of money and other gifts as a token of the New Year's greetings, and for the Emperor to despatch in return his envoys to the Yedo Castle to inquire after the Shogun's health. On such occasions the Shogun's Government appointed customarily from among the daimyô or feudal lords, three hundred in number, two officers to attend on the Imperial envoys. Strange as it may seem, it was customary that the daimyô thus appointed entertainers had not only to try their hardest to discharge their duties but also to defray all the entertainment expenses out of their own pockets. Yet the appointment was considered to be a great honour.

It was officially announced in the second month of the fourteeth year of Genroku (1701) that the Emperor Higashi-yama and the Ex-Emperor Reigen would despatch three Court nobles to arrive in Yedo on the eleventh of March. Accordingly on the fourth of February, Asano-Takumino-kami, Lord of Akô in the Province of Harima, and Date-Sakyônosuke, Lord of Yoshida in the Province of Iyo, were appointed Official Entertainers, with Kira-Kôzukeno-suke, Grand Master of Ceremonies of the Shogun, as their adviser.

On the occasion of getting the appointment, Asano at once asked to be excused from the post, frankly confessing

9

that he was not versed in Court etiquette. But he was
told by one of the Shogun's councillors that no daimyô
were really conversant with such matters, and that if appointed they would learn how to discharge their duties by
consulting Kira, who was ready to help them; so that
Asano was obliged to accept the office though quite reluctantly. And at that fateful moment, pre-ordained of
Heaven, were set in train all those events which were to
lead up eventually to the destruction of the Lord of Akô,
the extinction of his house, and the death of all his faithful
retainers.

Now Kira-Kôzukenosuke, Grand Master of Ceremonies,
was a *hatamoto*, a member of the class below the daimyô,
with an income amounting only to half that of the lowest
of daimyô and hardly enough to enable him to live up to
his honourable position. Being thus in pecuniary need,
he used to avail himself of every opportunity, whenever
possible, of getting bribes from rich daimyô. This was an
almost open secret, winked at rather leniently as a fault
that a man in his circumstances was apt to commit. But
as usual with a man of such habits, Kira was mean and
avaricious, and when crossed was malicious to a degree.

The best opportunity Kira had for turning affairs to his
own great profit was just such an occasion as the present
one, when his advice was most urgently needed. And on
the appointment of two daimyô unused to these ceremonies,
he must surely have smiled to himself and counted on his
ship coming in full laden.

As Date, Lord of Yoshida, was quite young, his experienced councillors managed everything for their master;
and knowing well Kira's greedy disposition, they made

him such costly presents as might be supposed to satisfy
and even exceed his anticipations.   It was then but natural
that he should expect much more from the other lord,
Asano, who was in a higher class of daimyô and therefore
wealthier than Date.   But there came no presents from
him save a box of dried bonito, which, though a formal
symbol of congratulation, cost only a mere trifle.   No
wonder the miserly Kira should get extremely angry at
this and take it as an unpardonable insult to himself, which
must be retaliated.

Asano heard of Date's splendid presents to Kira beforehand, but he was a man naturally averse to bribery and now
all the more so because he thought the occasion too solemn
for such petty tricks.   Nevertheless he might have shut his
eyes to the doings of his councillors staying with him in
Yedo if they had thought wise to follow the example of the
other party.   They, however, were men badly wanting in
worldly wisdom, knowing only how to wait on thier
master's pleasure, and let the chance go by without doing
anything more than presenting ordinary compliments to
Kira.

Things began to go at cross purposes, and when Asano
asked courteously for Kira's assistance, he was told unexpectedly to do as he thought fit, for Kira was, so the latter
averred, no better acquainted with the ceremonies than
Asano himself.   But pressing further in spite of the apparent ill-nature of this response, he was informed that
the best way to entertain the Imperial envoys was to send
them presents every day!   Asano on his part was too
dull-witted to see what his adviser was hinting at and went
at once to one of the Shogun's councillors to ascertain the

truth of this—which was, of course, flatly denied. This
in its turn reached the ears of Kira, who was angered still
more and vowed to make Asano commit blunders and fall
into disgrace.

Several things happened immediately before and after
the arrival of the Imperial envoys in Yedo which, all through
the purposely wrong advice of Kira, drove Asano into
extreme embarrassment and vexation. But he bore it with
all the patience he could muster, though bitterly hating and
cursing in his heart the foxy Kira. And at any rate two days
out of the three in which he was to attend on the noble
guests passed smoothly, and now arrived the final and most
momentous day of reception, the fourteenth of March, 1701.

It was the day on which the Shogun Tsunayoshi was to
present a reply to the Imperial messages, and the Grand
State Hall in the castle where the ceremony was to take
place was in readiness by ten in the morning with all high
personages attending in full uniform. The Official Entertainers and Masters of Ceremonies were waiting in the
corridor outside for the Imperial envoys to appear. All
was solemn and quiet, and everything seemed to be moving
on without a hitch, when Asano as Senior Entertainer
blurted out an awkward question, inquiring of the Grand
Master of Ceremonies whether he should receive the envoys
at the top or bottom of the entrance flight of steps.

The stupidity of the question, which a child might have
asked, made Kira laugh sarcastically as he expressed his
surprise at finding one ignorant of such a little matter
filling so important a post. And this in the hearing of all
about Asano! He felt his blood boiling with shame and
rage, but managed still to control himself. In gloomy

mood he had now nothing to do but watch the Junior
Entertainer Date, who was in Kira's favour, and take hints
from him,—an ignominous position he could hardly have
borne but for the importance of the occasion—when he
was accosted by Kajiwara-Yosôbei whom the Shogun's
mother had sent to request him to let her know for her
convenience as soon as possible when the ceremony was
finished.   Kajiwara addressed him particularly, and Asano
feeling very happy that the other understood him to be the
proper man for getting information from, gladly complied
with the request.   Kajiwara was going away, when Kira
stopped him and said aloud : " What arrangements are
you making with him ?   If you have anything to ask, let
me know.   That fellow Asano knows nothing of etiquette,
no, not one point of it."

On hearing this gross insult, which the pride of a samurai
could never tolerate, Asano lost his temper.   He forgot
everything,—place, time, and even himself : and when he
came to his senses, he found that he had struck Kira with
his sword, missed killing him, and was in the firm grip of
someone who was holding him.   That was Kajiwara, a
man of unusual physical strength, and frantic as he was,
Asano could do nothing in his arms.   Kira, astonished and
petrified with terror, attempted no resistance, on which
account he escaped with only slight wounds.   He was soon
carried away from the spot where he had fallen, and when
Asano saw that all was over with him, he handed over his
sword, and resigned himself to his fate, with but a single
exclamation of baffled rage.

He saw everything clearly, but did not repent his act.
He might have done so to some extent if he had accom-

plished his end and so had found relief for his temper, but being still excited, he thought himself absolutely justified. Insulted as he was, anybody with a particle of pride in himself would have done as he had ! What cared he if his house was exterminated and if he was ordered to commit *seppuku* (disembowelment) ? All this was nothing where justice was concerned. So his thoughts ran while he was kept in custody during the ceremony. And indeed, among those who were on the scene of the attack, there were more who sympathized with Asano than with Kira.

But there was one man who was extremely angry with Asano, and that was the Shogun Tsunayoshi, who felt that defiling with blood in such wise the auspiciousness of the occasion, on which he as central figure hoped to acquit himself with credit and honour, was an unpardonable offence deserving any punishment. He made up his mind to crush Asano under foot like a worm, for Asano was a mere nothing in his eye. But at any rate he had now to proceed with the ceremony, which with a change of place was duly brought to an end.

Both parties were now examined. On being questioned, Asano apologized for what he had done, careless of his high office and the nature of the occasion. But he had made, he said, an attack on Kira because of the unbearable insults repeatedly offered him. He simply could not help doing so. He was now prepared to receive any punishment for it, and he felt that by this frank avowal he had recovered his manliness. The conduct of Kira, on examination, elicited approval. In the summing-up of his case he was told that he had done well in not forgetting the place and occasion, and that, nothing blamable being found

in his conduct, it was the august pleasure of the Shogun
that he should do his best to nurse his wounds. So he
was allowed to go home, getting credit for his inability to
resist !

Asano was then placed in the custody of Tamura-Sakyôdayû, Lord of Ichinoseki, to whose mansion in Atago-
shita he was taken, clad in a disgraceful hempen dress and
seated in an unsightly palanquin over which a net was
thrown—a shameful advertisement to the public of its contents, a criminal !

Soon the Shogun summoned all his councillors to his
palace to have his command executed on Asano. His
mind had already been made up, and he simply said that
inasmuch as Asano, though on duty as Official Entertainer,
caused a disturbance in the palace by giving vent to private
resentment and thereby defiled the ceremonial hall, he
should be commanded to commit *seppuku* on that very day.
The councillors were all surprised to hear the Shogun's
intention as settled, and though knowing him to be as
wilful as a spoilt child, some of them pleaded at least for
respite in order to get a fair judgement for both sides ; but
all in vain. Ill-pleased with the councillors' hesitation,
the Shogun withdrew and made it known that his command was not to be disobeyed.

The Shogun's order to commit *seppuku* was at once
communicated to Asano in Tamura's mansion. Asano
knew this was to be and hoped only to die honourably.
But now, though ready to meet his death, he had one wish,
and that was to convey to someone the justness of what he
had done, so that he should not be misunderstood afterwards. So he asked for permission to write a letter to his

retainers in Akô.   In answer to this, it was suggested that
his message should be taken down instead, to which he
agreed, desiring the letter to be sent to his retainer Kataoka-
Gengoyemon or Isogai-Jûrôzayemon.   Asano dictated at
some length, but his custodian, shortened it simply to
this :

"I have no time to let you know in full what had
happened this morning, but it was a matter quite inevitable, though you might think it strange."

This was Asano's only dying message, but in those few
simple words, Ôishi and others read afterwards what had
wrung their master's heart, and they wept.

Kataoka-Gengoyemon to whom Asano wanted to have
his message sent was his favourite head-page.   He was a
faithful, trustworthy man, and when the news of the extraordinary incident reached his ears like a thunderbolt as
he stood at the gate of the castle where he had been waiting
for his master's return, he saw that it was a matter of grave
concern to the family and rode back immediately to Asano's
mansion at Teppôzu.   And after imparting the news to
the people there, he was quick enough to write a letter to
Akô reporting the matter and send it out by express messengers.   But feeling very anxious for his master's welfare,
he ran to Tamura's mansion to get further news about him,
when to his great sorrow he was told of the sentence passed and was handed his master's last message.   Though
thoroughly prepared for the worst, he felt the iron entering his soul.   Thinking for a while what to do, he took the
liberty of asking for permission to see his master for the
last time even for a moment, for that was now his only
wish, for which he would fain give his life.   The request

being fortunately granted, he was led to the garden and made to wait in front of a verandah. With a throbbing heart, he sat down on the ground in a reverential posture, when the sliding-screen was softly opened and a nobleman appeared. He was Asano-Takuminokami, his own dear lord, to whom he had pledged his life. At first sight his heart was choked and tears rushed to his eyes so that he prostrated himself without a word. Asano was moved, too, and said in a tearful voice, " You are welcome, Gengo." That was all he could say. Kataoka could only prostrate himself yet lower, his mind meanwhile being made up quickly to avenge his master's wrongs at any cost. He looked up and their eyes met. There was anger in them at first, then smiles. Each understood the other, and at that instant, Asano felt himself completely released from all fear of death. " Peace be with you, my lord." That was Kataoka's first and last words, and as he bowed, the sliding-screen was closed by the men in charge.

The day was now drawing to a close and the deep sound of a temple bell striking six trembled in the air. After a short ceremony in which the head inspector solemnly sentenced Asano to *seppuku*, the latter was led to the garden where all preparations had been made. On the ground were spread a few coarse sheets of matting on which a couple of regular mats covered with a rug were laid. Asano saw at once that the seat was unworthy of himself, for never before had a daimyô been made to commit *seppuku* in the open air, but it was now no time for protest. He calmly sat on the rug and asking for paper and writing-brush, wrote down a farewell ode which ran :—

> " Frailer far than the tender flowers
>   That are soon scattered by the wind,
> Must I now bid a last farewell
>   And leave the genial spring behind ? " [1]

He then opened his breast and was about to touch his body with a dagger when the assistant beheaded him from behind. He was in his thirty-fifth year. The cherry-blossoms in the garden were fully blown and in the silence that pervaded the place, some petals were wafted by the breeze as if to mourn over the passing of a proud samurai.

Everything now seemed to be finished : but everything was far from being finished. The death of Asano, Lord of Akô, was only the beginning of everything that was to follow.

THE SURRENDER OF THE AKÔ CASTLE

Asano-Takuminokami was dead : but his wife and his retainers were living. They all knew that their master had come to an untimely end while Kira, whose outrageous insults had brought things to such a pass, had been acquitted, and praised into the bargain. And on the house of Asano severe punishments, con-comittant to that capital one of *seppuku*, were inflicted one after another,—confiscation of property and extinction of the family name. Besides all the retainers had to be turned out and deprived of their living allowances. No wonder that they were all deeply angered. But the mansion at Teppôzu and the villa in Shibuya being ordered to be surrendered on the very evening of the *seppuku*, they were too busy now to think of themselves.

---

1   The translation is by Jûkichi Inouye.

Lady Asano, a beautiful young woman of high birth, was a samurai's wife as well. Though at first she almost fainted from the shock at the news of her husband's bloodshed, she soon recovered her composure and was prepared to accept her fate. She knew her husband had been being insulted by Kira so that she could feel well his mortification at his failure to take vengeance. If she had been a man . . . ! But she had now to bestir herself, too, seeing first of all to have the things removed from her late dear husband's room.

When the furniture and other things were all taken away, the empty house looked gaunt and ghostly in the flickering light of sparse candles, and the people moving about as in a funeral were like shadowy spectres. In the silence they felt as if the voice of their late lord might be heard somewhere in the dark. And now as the men waited speechless for the officers coming to take over the mansion, they all looked at one another vowing vengeance in their hearts. They were men brought up in the teaching that if one's lord should be insulted, one must in loyalty die for him. Their lord had not only suffered insult, but had lost his life ; how much more then, they thought, must they suffer for him, not merely die ? Indeed, though there were some among them who turned out to be black sheep after all, yet such men staying then in Yedo as Kataoka-Gengoyemon, Isogai-Jûrôzayemon, Hara-Sôyemoñ, Horibe-Yahyôye, and Horibe-Yasubyôye, not only remained true to the last, but proved to be staunch members of that famous band of forty-seven.

Akô being near Himeji, it took formerly almost five days for express couriers to cover the distance of about 387

miles between Yedo and that place, so that the first messengers who left Yedo at eleven on the morning of March
14th reached Akô at ten on the evening of the 18th, and the
second messengers appeared at six the next morning.
With their arrival the whole tragedy became clearly known.
Ôishi-Kuranosuke, chief councillor in charge of the castle,
who had been praying that nothing might go amiss with
his lord in discharging his duty, was, of course, greatly
astonished at this horrible news ; but with great presence
of mind, he lost no time in summoning all the retainers of
Akô, some three hundred in number, to an extraordinary
meeting to discuss what steps they should take at that grave
moment.

Ôishi's mind was made up at once.   He saw clearly the
proper course of action that a samurai should take in such
a case, but he knew, too, that he must use sense and tact
even in coming to that inevitable step of taking revenge,
which he saw would need many hands to accomplish.

At the first meeting Hara-Sôyemon, one of the second
messengers, reported the matter, enumerating the many
occasions on which their lord had swallowed the insults
given by Kira, till he would have looked like a chicken-
hearted samurai if he had not at last taken offence and struck.
He also told of the chagrin of all his fellow retainers in
Yedo at seeing their lord ordered to commit *seppuku* without
any trial and that, too, on matting spread on the ground
like a commoner, while Kira had been left alone.   At his
heated words even Ôishi grew excited and asked if such
a disgrace could be put up with.   " No " was the general
cry ; " Revenge ! Revenge ! " shouted most of the three
hundred gathered there.

Ôishi heard those shouts with pleasure, but, of course, he could not rush blindly into action at once. He must make sure that each retainer who gave voice to this opinion was really ready for it. Besides there might be steps which ought to be taken before that last desperate one. So he asked Ôno, his fellow councillor, who was known for his cleverness in managing clan affairs, what his opinion was. Ôno thought that loyalty did not consist alone in offering one's life, and that the proper course they should take first at that moment was to appeal for the continuance of the house of their lord inasmuch as his younger brother Asano-Daigaku might be recommended as his heir.

Ôishi agreed without hesitation that this was quite proper, and, in spite of a general outburst of discontent, proceeded to give his opinion to the effect that in doing so it was best to put on a bold front to show that they were no weaklings that could be beaten into any shape at the pleasure of the Shogunate.

Loud shouts of assent rose in many places. But Ôno was for no resistance. That would excite the other party all the more, he thought; it was better to curry favour with them at that moment. "Then there are," he went on to say, "our own interests to consider."

But the youthful among them would not let him speak on. "Now that our lord has committed *seppuku*," they said, "we have no time to spend idling about the question of our interests."

"Yes," said Ôishi, as if to side with Ôno, "the question of interests is sometimes quite important. For instance, it is our duty at this juncture to protect the interests of

the people of our castle-town as much as possible. But,"
and he changed his tone, " we samurai should not take our
own interests into consideration. Our path is straight :
we must show our mettle. You know our motto, ' When
his master is insulted, the vassal dies.' Now is the time to
follow it. No one is here, I hope, who holds life dear."

" Never ! Never ! " shouted some.

" But," he went on, " there may be some here to whom
life is everything. Let them do as they like. Only, *we*
are not going to surrender this castle meekly."

Ôno and his supporters had something more to say in
their defence, and the heated discussion did not end by
sunset. So the meeting had to be adjourned without
coming to any decision.

That evening Ôishi had a talk with Yoshida-Chûzayemon
and Hara-Sôyemon. They were the two whom Ôishi
admitted to his confidence from the first. Yoshida was
a cool-headed, thoughtful man and, though never obtru-
sive, had always good suggestions to make. Hara, on the
other hand, was passionate, and trusting Ôishi thoroughly
would do anything for his sake.

" I can never breathe freely," said Ôishi, " until Kira's
head is cut off."

" Nor I," agreed Hara at once.

" I agree with you," said Yoshida, " but I think our
first duty is to work for the restoration of our lord's
house."

" That's true too," said Ôishi.

" If his brother Daigaku were a little firmer in character
. . . " sighed Hara.

" No use regretting it now," said Ôishi. " But we

must try what we can do. And in doing so, nothing is
more important than to show that we would stick at
nothing if our wishes were ignored."

" You are right. They hold us too cheap."

" So I'm going to propose that we should stand a
siege. That, too, will serve to show us who are cowards
and who not. The Ôno interests, I'm sure, will withdraw. If that is not enough, I will suggest committing
seppuku as a stronger way of protest. I can then unbosom myself to those who still stick to the cause."

" That's a good idea," said Hara eagerly.

" What do you think, Yoshida ? "

" I think so too."

" To tell the truth, I hated to die. It's quite strange,
but since I heard of our lord committing *seppuku*, I've
come to think nothing of following his example."

" His death has made us all brave."

" To live up to our principles. How say you ? "

" To be sure."

And so they parted, vowing to fight it out.

For two more days the serious conference lasted, to
decide on measures best suited to the occasion, which
shows how obstinately the opposing sides headed by Ôishi
and Ôno respectively crossed words one with the other.
They agreed on the point of appealing to the Shogunate
that Asano's brother be allowed to succeed the late lord
as his heir, but Ôishi was for backing that appeal with a
strong determination to hold the castle and fight to the last
in its defence, while Ôno thought it would be disrespectful
to authority. To appeal while holding the castle by force
would be in his opinion tantamount to rising in revolt

against the Shogun. It would be an unpardonable mad-
ness, dishonouring the fame of their late loyal lord. "We
cannot then," he concluded, " but surrender the castle
first and disbanding ourselves ask for the special favour to
appoint the heir."

Thus Ôno argued plausibly in order to make good his
escape.

It was then that Ôishi advanced his great opinion.

" Sir Ôno's argument is entirely wrong," said he.
" What a samurai should stand to is his honour, honour
to discharge what he is called to do. It is a sin and a
shame that, forgetting his part at this great moment, he
should propose to do nothing but hesitate, fear death,
and try to escape from it. Who can tell whether our
petition if sent in might be granted ? And what would
the world say if we left our castle readily with that
uncertain hope as a pretext? Would it solace our hearts
to hear it said in future days that among the samurai of
the Akô Clan, after several generations of discipline, not
one man was found to lay down his life at the supreme
crisis ? Standing a siege and fighting to the last might
be little help to our clan, but is it not far better than
staining the fame of our late lord and his ancestors by
any mean conduct ? "

At this all the brave retainers cheered him, while the
worldly-wise were mostly reduced to silence. But Ôno
still said this and that, trying to stem the tide, when Hara
rose, seated himself before him, and pulling himself up,
said :

" Hold your tongue. We who are here are all of
Councillor Ôishi's opinion. If you disagree, you needn't

stay here any longer. Be gone at once."

Cowed by the grim determination of Hara, who spoke
hand on sword, Ôno could do nothing but withdraw
moodily, and with him all his party sneaked away.

There was now no one left who opposed Ôishi's proposal, and it was soon resolved that it should be adopted
and that they should despatch two delegates to Yedo to
file the petition with the Shogunate.

It was soon rumoured that the Akô retainers were going
to stand a siege. Those were the prosperous days of
Genroku, about a hundred years after the establishment of
the Tokugawa Shogunate, and absolute peace had reigned
over the country so long that people were eager to have
some unusual happenings to talk about. The news of
Lord Asano's violence and shedding of blood at the Castle
of Yedo, followed by his *seppuku*, was received with much
interest, making all people think ill of Kira. So it was no
wonder they should now hear with delight of the bold step
taken by those concerned and even anticipate to their great
satisfaction that the Akô warriors might show some
miraculous valour in dispelling the besieging forces gathering from far and near. They were, however, mostly those
people who lived far from Akô. The town people did
not, of course, wish the struggle to take on too desperate
a character, and even among the retainers, the greater part
of them did not like the strong step decided on. Of course,
they did not say openly they disliked it because life was too
dear to them. But they all ascribed their dislike to the cool,
self-confident attitude assumed by Ôishi at the conference,
so they said, as if he thought he alone could manage everything. What a pretext, to be sure!

There were, however, some who, hearing of the stand made by the loyalists, made haste to join them. They were those retainers who had stayed in Yedo or elsewhere in the service of their lord, or who for some reason or other had severed their connections with the Akô Clan and were turning *rônin* (masterless samurai). But not all of these were admitted. Especially the *rônin* were given a polite refusal in spite of their earnest entreaty, for otherwise the Akô retainers would, in Ôishi's opinion, gain ill repute for offering resistance to the Shogunate by gathering outsiders. And even the proper retainers were not easily accepted if they did not concur *in toto* with Ôishi in his present attitude. Kataoka and Isogai, who had been in special favour with their lord in Yedo and were loyal to the bottom of their hearts, came back to Akô hastily and went to see Ôishi. They were for taking revenge and not for such a passive step as standing a siege. But as Ôishi took no notice of what they said, they grew moody and rarely showed themselves at the castle. He was, of course, one with them at heart, but to all outward appearance pretended to be ready to die in defence of the castle. He thought that now was too early a time even to mention the final step, and so made fools of them. Seeing them offended, Ôishi smiled inwardly, feeling more assured that they were trustworthy fellows.

Previous to the arrival at Yedo of the delegates, the Shogunate appointed Government officers to have the Akô Castle surrendered and began to press hard on the matter; and its assault by military force became imminent. It was now no time to delay and Ôishi convened another conference, ostensibly to discuss matters relating to standing

a siege. Hearing that there were many applicants to the
league from Yedo and elsewhere, the younger members
expected that they would have a large meeting that day.
But only some sixty had assembled by the appointed hour.
They waited for some little time, but no others showed up.
They were rather astonished at this great decrease in their
number, from more than three hundred present on the
first occasion to just sixty-one now !   To those seriously
minded to fight to the last in defence of their castle, this
state of affairs was something of a wet blanket.   But Ôishi
was not disappointed ; he would indeed have been so if
he had really intended to hold the castle.   But as his
ultimate object was to take revenge, he was fully confident
that he could attain it with that number present.   And
he looked with pleasure at the faces of the determined,
reliable men sitting about him.

All were now waiting for Ôishi to speak.   And among
those who waited was seen a mere stripling of sixteen on
the one hand, and a grey-headed man of over seventy on
the other.

" Are any more men coming ? "

" I'm afraid not," said Hara.   " It seems a great many
have suddenly fallen ill."

All laughed at the joke but soon became silent as the
grave as Ôishi spoke thus :

" It gives me great pleasure to see you all come here
to-day, remembering the obligations you owe to the house
of Asano.   We must now do our best to requite them
along the lines we resolved upon the other day.   But to
be frank, I am afraid we cannot hope to do very much
with such a small number.   Even with all the retainers in

the clan, we might not hope to hold out so long as a
month, besieged as we shall be with forces ever so many
times as large as ours.   How much less then can we do
with only sixty of us ?   It is very well to try to stand the
siege, but if we were defeated in one day, we should become only a butt for ridicule.   As things have come to
such a pass, there is no help for it but to resort to another
course of action.   In my opinion we might earnestly entreat
the Government officers who are coming soon, to assist in
the restoration of our lord's house, and if they refuse we
could redeem our vain efforts by all committing *seppuku*
in this hall.   That would awaken the sympathy of the
Shogunate and lead eventually to the accomplishment of
our object.   I should like to hear what you all think of it."

The men looked surprised at this unexpected speech of
Ôishi and did not know what to say, when Hara said in
a loud voice :   " What Councillor Ôishi says is very true.
We all place our lives in his hands.   At his bidding I'll
be the first to commit *seppuku*."   To this Yoshida added
his approval, and the motion was unanimously carried.

" Then let us form a league now," said Ôishi, " and
sign our names to this joint note."

And he took reverentially out of his cloth-wrapper
some sheets of paper on the first of which a solemn pledge
was already written.   The men were surprised at his
readiness.

Ôishi was the first to sign his name and seal it with his
blood, after which the others began to follow suit.   But
when the paper went round to a boy by the name of Yatô-
Yemonshichi, Ôishi made him wait, and asked of his father
Yatô-Chôsuke the age of the boy.   Being told that the boy

was only sixteen, he praised his courage but advised him, as he was too young, to keep out of the league for the sake of his house. The boy's father was about to speak, but Yemonshichi could not hold his tongue.

"I am surprised to hear that from you, Councillor Ôishi," said he. "I served the late lord as boy-page and was much in his favour. I have offered him my life and am not a bit behind others in loyalty. As my father has made up his mind to die, so have I done. Please let me walk in the path of faithfulness with everyone here ; I have no mind to be left behind."

At this everyone was moved to tears and felt very proud to have such a brave boy among them. Ôishi thought of his son, Chikara by name, who though only fourteen years old was also wanting to follow him to death, and felt that he read now his son's heart in the boy's pleading. And knowing that he must grant Chikara's wishes after all, he gladly accepted Yemonshichi on his father's approval to be one of the members.

When everyone had finished signing his name, a servant named Mimura-Jirôzayemon came in. He was a brawny, clumsy fellow, though looking simple and good at heart. As he appeared someone hurriedly hid the paper. At once Mimura felt insulted and trembling with anger, said :

"I am a man of low position, but I don't think I'm lacking in fidelity ; yet you try to hide the paper from me in all haste as if I were a spy. How can you cut me to the heart by such insulting treatment ? "

And he wept bitterly.

Ôishi saw the man's sincerity and invited him to join the league, to which he gladly agreed with many thanks.

When he signed his name at the very end, he wept again, but this time in the fulness of his heart.   He was the man, indeed, who on that memorable night of heroic retribution about a year and a half after, burst open the back gate of Kira's mansion with his heavy mallet.

The signed paper now brought to Ôishi, he took it up reverentially and read aloud the names one by one, to which the men listened solemnly with new determination to defy death.

"I am deeply moved," said he when he had finished reading, "to see you pledge yourselves so willingly to our cause and feel now free to make no secret of what I have in mind.   We know that things have come to this pass all because our late lord, rightly offended at the insults to which he was subjected by Kira, was just inadvertent enough to strike him in the palace.   If Kira had been killed then, we should have nothing to say now. But he not merely escaped only slightly wounded, but also got praised for his cowardice.   Think of the unfairness of it!   Kira, the enemy of our lord, is also *our* enemy.   To die now following our lord to the grave would be very well, but how much better would it be to do so after satisfying his resentment by killing Kira? I asked you to pledge yourselves to commit *seppuku*, only because I wanted to find out trustworthy men to whom I might unbosom myself of my true purpose.   Now I know your sincerity; if we are united and try to avenge our lord on Kira, I have no doubt that we shall succeed. What do you think about it?"

This speech was, of course, greeted with shouts of joy. The announcement fell upon them just like the sun suddenly bursting through the gloomy clouds. Most of them felt much relieved. They were now not merely to die, but were given an enemy to kill. Everyone hated Kira, detested him as an abomination. And they felt their courage mounting tenfold.

Only one or two old men among them hesitated to join hands with the others. But as their reason was that they feared they might not live till they had attained their object, which seemed to be a very long way off, they were soon set at ease by Ôishi, Yoshida, and others who assured them that their fears were no obstacle to their joining a league whose members were to act in a body and not separately. So the men allied themselves in this new secret league, the object of which was not to be divulged even to their relatives or friends.

The two delegates sent to Yedo started from Akô on the 25th of March and arrived at their destination on the 4th of April. They went quite slowly from the start. They were to hand over the petition to the Government officers Araki and Sakakibara who were appointed to receive the surrender of the Akô Castle, but were baffled at finding that they had already left for Akô on the 27th of the previous month. Without knowing what to do, they went to consult with Fujii and Yasui, councillors of Asano in Yedo and their acquaintances, forgetting that they had been told not to see them. The councillors, who were of a peace-at-any-price policy, were astonished to hear of what the men in Akô were intending to do and took the delegates to see Lord Toda, a powerful daimyô and cousin to Lord Asano. Toda, who had been displeased at the rash act of Asano, feared very much that the new

development might involve his house in trouble and said
in an offended tone that such a reckless petition should not
be filed with the Shogunate. He wrote at once a strong
letter to Ôishi, advising him to desist from the step and
surrender the castle as ordered without causing any trouble,
for that would accord, so he said, with the cherished wishes
of his late lord who served the Shogun with utmost
obedience. The matter was also communicated to Asano-
Daigaku, who joined with Toda in advising the delegates
not to take so injudicious a step, so the latter could do
nothing but come back to report what they had been told.

The delegates made haste this time and were in Akô on
the 11th before the Government officers arrived. Ôishi
was not surprised that they had failed, for he had slyly
contrived that the matter should fall out in this very way by
appointing men as delegates who were well acquainted with
Councillors Fujii and Yasui. His plan worked almost too
well ; and though displeased on the one hand with the
wording of Toda's letter and the falsity of tone in which he
commended his cousin's merits, he was glad on the other
to find a very good reason for surrendering the Akô
Castle peacefully.

Another conference was to be convened, and this was
done on the very day of the return of the delegates. Its
attendance, however, was just as large as on the first
occasion, as this was a safe one, touching no questions of
dying fighting or committing *seppuku*, but also an important
one, for it was to decide each one's share in the distribution
of money in winding up the affairs of the clan.

As soon as the meeting was opened, Ôishi, assuming a
troubled book, said that they were placed in an awkward

position and read aloud Toda's letter, reporting the advice
sent by Daigaku as well. " Now that things have come to
this," he went on, " we are very sorry, but there seems to
be no help for it but to follow their advice. If we dared
stand a siege in defiance of them, Sir Daigaku might not be
free from the responsibility. We do not wish him to be
involved in any way, so I want to have our former resolution cancelled and surrender our castle without any more
ado. I like to know what you say to it."

" I support," said Hara immediately, " Councillor Ôishi's
opinion."

There was no one who contradicted it, and Ôishi's
proposal was carried.

Ôno and his party were bewildered at the swiftness of
this decision, but as the matter was settled to their liking,
they felt extremely at ease. Ôno was emboldened to have
his say :

" Didn't I say so from the first ? But there are many
arrangements to make in surrendering the castle ; how
do you propose to go about them ? "

" We would like to leave all such matters to Councillor
Ôishi."

" We all agree."

Thus Ôno was not given an opportunity to make any
proposal and the meeting was adjourned till another time.

Ôno and his friends felt disgusted at the apostacy of
Ôishi and his supporters and thought them shamelessly
making themselves ridiculous. But the latter nursing their
secret proudly only smiled and looked forward to the day
when they would astound the cowards.

The next day, April 12th, was wholly spent in making

various arrangements for surrender. Ôishi directed every-thing. First an inventory of all the arms and furniture in the castle had to be made. Secondly cleaning up the castle and repairing the roads and bridges in the district must be attended to. And thirdly all the clan paper-money circulating among the people must be exchanged for specie. The last item was the most difficult to execute, for such paper-money had been issued in great excess under Ôno's administration. Ôishi found that it could be converted into silver at 60 per cent of the face value[1] and announced to that effect. This was more than the people had hoped for and they welcomed the declaration with much joy. They did not know, they said, that they had such an excellent councillor in the clan. No doubt the castle was admirably cleaned up, the roads and bridges repaired and swept most neatly, but the tidying up of the loose administration by converting this over-issue must be said to have been the most noteworthy of all.

On the following day, April 13th, the question of distri-buting the money in the clan among the retainers was discussed. In the centre of the castle hall, a heap of money amounting to 16,400 ryô in gold and silver, the remnants from the coffers, was shown to view. The men assembled glanced furtively at the heap, pretending not to see it. Even when one's lord had committed *seppuku* and his castle was about to be delivered up, gold had a fascinating hold on one's heart, and most of the men could not help calculating secretly what their shares would be. Especially

---

1. This was more strictly the conversion into silver at the rate of 600 ryô per one *kan* (3.75 kilogrammes) of paper-money, the ryô being a unit of old Japanese coinage.

Ôno and his son and some others were jealous to guard their interests. Ôishi did not like to have the management of this disagreeable affair, but he could not escape it, and, intending to deal with it fairly, announced first of all such reductions to be made as were necessitated by the circumstances. First there were donations to be made to the family temple of Asano and others connected thereto, that religious services for their lord's house might not be discontinued. Then the dowry of their lord's widow, now divorced, had to be sent back to her. These two were matters of course, to which no one protested. There was, however, one more thing to be considered, Ôishi said. And this was the reserve funds for the restoration of the house of Asano. Ôno and others were vexed, thinking that it was a useless provision for things that might not in all probability come to pass, but could not oppose the proposal openly, for that would be flat disloyalty. So it was approved by a unanimous vote. These funds, let it be noted, when their use was finally precluded, were appropriated by Ôishi for carrying out the scheme of revenge.

The money left after all these reductions were made amounted to some 6,400 *ryô*, and this was to be distributed now. In the opinion of the democratic Ôishi, this ought be divided equally among the three hundred and odd retainers then in Akô, for those who lived on small stipends suffered more by their loss than those higher-salaried ones who had some savings and property to be disposed of. But Ôno, thinking that it would be too much to be turned away with only 20 *ryô*, at once raised an objection to this, saying that one's expenses differed with one's status so that the most reasonable way of distribution would be to do so proportionately to the amount of one's stipend. His opinion was vigorously supported only by his party, but as men in the lower stations hesitated to say anything for themselves, Ôishi took it to be the general view and decided in its favour. And the rate of distribution was fixed at 24 *ryô* per 100 *koku*.[1]

Ôishi ordered Okajima-Yasoyemon, treasurer of the clan, to count out the share of each retainer and pay him on the spot. So he first took out Ôishi's share amounting to 350 *ryô* and brought it him. Ôishi, however, declined to take it, saying that as he had some savings, he desired it to be distributed among those whose stipends were below 100 *koku*. This was from no false pride on his part but he really meant it. Next came Ôno whose share amounting to about 200 *ryô* was pocketed with a rather bad grace, for it turned out to fall a good deal short of his first expectation. And so on till all the money was cleared away.

After the meeting was over, Ôno turned to one of his set and said grumblingly :

" I'm suspicious of that fellow Okajima. Who knows but that he has made free with some of the clan's money ?"

Hearing this through an eavesdropper, Okajima, who prided himself on his integrity, got so much enraged that he went at once to see Ôno. His looks being so black, he was told that Ôno was out. " Then I'll see him later on," he said grimly, and called again after a while. Again he was told that Ôno was out. But undaunted by the refusal, he repeated his call till at last, saying that he would wait for Ôno, he tried to force his way in. A desperate situa-

---

1. A samurai's stipend used to be paid by the year in the form of rice measured by the *koku*. One *koku* is equal to 4.9629 bushels.

tion this; the usher, stopping him for a moment, ran off
to ask what to do and coming back said apologetically :

" The master has gone to bed with a sudden illness.
He asks you kindly to come again to-morrow morning."

" Well then," said Okajima, " his life is spared till
to-morrow.   I've nothing to do with a sick person.
Your master seems to fall suddenly ill so often.   Ha,
ha ! "

When Okajima called again the next morning, he found
to his surprise that Ôno and his son had secretly decamped
in the night.   And in ɑoing so, they were shameless enough
to leave behind the son's baby sleeping with its nurse for
fear of attracting notice by its crying !

The day for the surrender of the castle was drawing near.
Some time previous to this the Shogunate, as we have
seen, appointed Araki and Sakakibara as the officers to
take delivery of the castle, but they were merely civil
officers to assist the chief or army officers, Wakizaka, Lord
of Tatsuno in the Province of Harima, and Kinoshita, Lord
of Ashimori in the Province of Bitchû, who were coming
with their forces ready to give battle in case of emergency,
for it was feared that the Akô men might resist the orders
to the bitter end.   And, indeed, such was the fuss made by
the Shogunate that they even ordered the other lords in
the neighbouring districts to send their forces as reinforcements, too, so that the lonely castle would be surrounded
by coils and coils of these fighting men.   Ôishi knew all
this, but as the acceptance of the orders had been communicated to the officers, he had no cause to be overawed
and rather laughed in his sleeve at so much trouble being

taken by the Shogunate.   Still, so long as the castle was not delivered, it must be kept under strict watch, and Ôishi's instructions were so closely followed that not a spy was found within its grounds.

On April 18th, as it was reported that Araki and Sakaki-bara and their retinue had already reached the district of Akô, Ôishi and others went on horseback to receive them, and coming back before them, gave orders to make ready for them by opening the main gate of the castle.   Though they were assistant officers, as they were dispatched directly from the Yedo Government, their preliminary inspection had to be gone through.   At the castle they were again received by Ôishi, and all the important papers relating to administration, finance, and property were submitted for inspection.   After that they were taken by Ôishi all through the castle, which had been so neartly tidied and swept that not a speck of dust was found on its polished floors.   All important stations were guarded by armed warriors, who saluted the officers solemnly and with due courtesy as they passed, so that it was difficult to believe that those were doomed samurai remaining in a lordless castle.   They were so struck with this state of things that they felt very sorry that such a distinguished clan should be abolished and thrown away like trash, while they admired Ôishi's ex-ceptional ability in maintaining order and managing every-thing in a way quite worthy of the chief councillor of a clan.

By and by the officers were taken to the living room of the late Lord Asano.   Special care had been taken to keep this room beautiful as well as comfortable so that it looked as if its deceased occupant were still living.   The officers entered it ceremoniously and sat down, when Ôishi took out a petition and presenting it said :

" To-day we respectfully deliver to you this castle as ordered by the Shogunate. Our lord being dead and our clan abolished, we have no heart to meet you officers from the Government, living still as we do in the midst of this overwhelming calamity. But it is only because our lord's brother Daigaku might be allowed to inherit the house that we are living on, abiding our shame. As is well known, the first ancestor of the Asano house was under the special patronage of the Shogun Iyeyasu, and his line has enjoyed for a century an honourable position among the daimyô so that it is with hearts bursting with grief that we see it now become extinct. Our earnest supplication then at this juncture is that, as a special act of grace, Daigaku will be appointed successor in whatever small way seems fit. If this petition should be taken up and furthermore granted, it is then that we all will make away with ourselves before the grave of our lord and discharge our duty as retainers. If you sympathize with our situation, we sincerely beg of you to hand this petition to the Government and use your influence with the Councillors in our behalf."

Such being the place and the speech, the two officers could not help being moved. But as they could not answer officially, they merely nodded in silence.

When the officers returned to their appointed inn, Ôishi was sent for after a while, and a reply to his request was given privately by Araki. First he expressed his thanks for the trouble Ôishi had taken in receiving them by having the route neatly swept and the bridges repaired, and keeping order throughout the distinct, and admired the way in which the men at the castle behaved, all reflecting Ôishi's unremitting care in honouring the high commissioners. Then he proceeded to say that he had not been able to answer Ôishi's request in his official function, but as it was quite reasonable, they had sent a special messenger to Yedo carrying the petition. On returning they would do their best to have it granted; and so forth.

Ôishi thanked them for their kindness and felt much relieved, not because he saw a gleam of hope in the officers' sympathy, but because he had taken a proper step which justified his delay in following his lord to the grave. In his mind his course was always clear to him. But if perchance his wishes had been realized, that page of history inscribed with the thrilling episode of bloodshed known as the Akô vendetta would have been unwritten, and the Japanese would have missed a great drama called the *Chûshingura*; nevertheless no stain would have been on his or his followers' honour as samurai in merely putting an end to their lives and joining their lord in the other world, for thus their duty as subjects would have been performed to perfection.

That night was the last one for the Akô retainers to hold their castle and call it their own. So Ôishi gave them orders to keep strict watch over it and keep it safe from fire and disturbance. And they all sat up, grudging every minute as it passed away. Presently near dawn a trumpet-conch was heard blown somewhere in the distance. Ôishi went up the castle-tower alone to take a last look at his beloved country. The stars were twinkling brightly in the sky, and the castle-town was still a sea of darkness in which the roofs were scarcely distinguishable. In a southerly direction he saw a long line of torches coming down the Takatori Pass and across the River Chigusa, and approaching the town. They were, of course, those forces of several clans in Himeji and Okayama ordered out for reinforcement. On close scrutiny he discerned in the town a force encamping for several blocks. These were the troops of Lord Wakizaka, Chief Commissioner. Again looking towards the sea, he saw there, floating like a shoal of whales on the rippling waves already whitening, warships from many clans guarding the coast. Ôishi stood looking at all this in the cool breeze of the dawn, growing never tired of it. Never had he dreamt that in all his life he should wait thus for the dawn. With an unspeakable feeling swelling in his breast, he eagerly gazed at the sight to get it deeply chiselled on his mind, so that if he were ever tempted to relax in his efforts in performing the one great task put on his shoulders, this should rise in a vision to stir him up to action by reminding him that once he had been dauntless enough to fight against such great odds if he had been but so minded, and so should he ever be.

At six o'clock in the morning, as the appointed hour had come, all the gates of the castle were opened for the chief and assistant officers to enter it with their men. Soon the new men changing places with the old ones, as the process of delivery was merely formal, everything went smoothly as pre-arranged. Presently Ôishi assembled together all his men and led them to the Kegakuji, the family temple of Asano, to report the matter to the ancestors sleeping there. On the face of it, it was but a simple ceremony without any elaborate ritual appropriate to the gravity of the occasion, but the silent tears everyone there shed as they bade farwell to the tombs and to one another were enough to burst the heart of any who could look deep into them and feel their full significance.

CHAPTER III

THE LOYAL RETAINERS OF AKÔ—II

ÔISHI AT YAMASHINA

As the Akô Clan was now extinguished all the retainers perforce turned *rônin* and dispersed, each going his separate way to wherever he might manage, somehow or other, to get a living. With those sixty-one who had pledged themselves to the secret league, and some others who, though of the same mind, were staying in Yedo and elsewhere at the time of the conferences, the same was, of course, the case ; and we may say that the places they settled in after a while were, roughly speaking, the three districts of Akô and its neighbourhood, Kyoto and Osaka, and Yedo. Ôishi had known that this would be so, and long before the surrender of the castle he had written to a relative of his in Kyoto to find for him a suitable place in its vicinity wherein to live in retirement, for he thought that that was about the most convenient place for him, as leader, to keep in touch with his men. To Yamashina, then, a small village just outside Kyoto to the east, he came up in July, three months after the break-up of the clan— having been delayed, mostly on account of a rather protracted illness—and began to lead a quiet life there.

To those who knew what Ôishi's main object in life was, his mode of existence at Yamashina must have appeared somewhat strange. It was all very well that he should have declined the many good offers made him by various daimyô who, seeing the great sagacity shown in his surrender of the Akô Castle, would have liked very

much to take him into their service. But here at Yamashina he not only bought a house and land, but also had
fine semi-detached rooms built on of the best materials,
with a beautiful garden in front in which some choice
varieties of peony, his favourite flower, were planted,—
all seeming to indicate his intention to settle there for life
and, by and by transferring the headship of his house to
his son Chikara, to enjoy the comforts of easy retirement.

To understand this puzzle aright, we must just glance
at what Kira was doing meanwhile. Seeing that capital
punishment in the form of *seppuku*, the confiscation of
castle and fief, and the extinction of the family line had all
been inflicted on Asano, while he himself had escaped
without even so much as a reprimand, he was not slow to
guess what rancour Asano's surviving retainers would
nurse against him. And being a great coward, he set
about at once to guard himself from danger. The antece-
dents of all those employed in his household were strictly
looked into, preference being given to those coming from
his fief in Mikawa. The gates of his residence were strongly
guarded, and no tradesmen were admitted into the premises, while all visitors and messengers were closely
watched. Kira had a great supporter in the person of
Lord Uesugi of Yonezawa, who was really his third son,
but had been adopted into that family, of which his wife
was a connection. Now the Yonezawa Clan was noted
for its bowmen, so that if Kira should be attacked by Akô
rônin and killed, it would at once reflect on the military
fame of the house of Uesugi. Hence its famous councillor
Chisaka did his utmost to defend Kira by sending to his
house selected warriors to be ready for any emergency.

That was why Ôishi went to such lengths in laying his
plans most carefully for the attack before he should deliver
it.   But all that was yet in the future.   In the meantime he
was beset on all sides by spies sent by Chisaka.   They
appeared even in Akô to ferret out Ôishi's real intention.
Now that he was at Yamashina, they were all the more
alert to watch him.   They prowled about his house, dogged
his steps, and even disguised themselves as workmen
among those he employed in building.   So it was but
natural that he should use every means to throw them off
the scent, and his fine, comfortable country seat was really
nothing but a deception put up to blind the sharp eyes of
the enemy.

Ôishi, however, did not remain idle in his seemingly
easy life.   In the northern part of Kyoto there was a temple called Reikôin which had some connection with the
founder of the Asano family.   The ground where it stood
was thickly wooded and quite secluded.   It struck Ôishi
at once that the place might in some way serve his purposes.
So he rented a little cloister belonging to the temple to use
for his lodgings whenever he was in Kyoto.   Then he
erected there a tomb in memory of his late master over the
latter's ceremonial dress, for the convenience of his men
living in that part of the country, who might wish to pay
their homage to their departed lord.   On the 14th of
August, the death-day of Asano, he called out as many of
his men as he could and held there a mass for the repose of
his master's soul, asking them all to come on the same day
every month after that to visit the grave.   There was
nothing about this to waken any suspicions, but Ôishi
and his men were thus able to come into frequent contact

with one another to keep their common flame burning in their breasts and have a word or two exchanged in helping their scheme forward.

A little previous to this Ôishi got a letter by a special messenger from Araki in Yedo, who had been, as we have seen, one of the Government officers appointed to take delivery of the Akô Castle. Araki seemed to have been deeply moved by Ôishi's manner and speech in requesting the restoration of the house of Asano, and, after reporting his mission, called privately on the Councillors one by one and conveyed to them Ôishi's sincere wishes. As that was the first time that such a request from Ôishi had reached their ears, they listened to it with the greatest attention, and some even said that it would demand their special consideration in the future. The letter was a report of all this and purported to be little else. But it was very significant, in showing how much Araki felt himself concerned about Ôishi's request. Ordinarily, a man in a high position such as his, being Superintendent Officer, would never condescend to write to his subordinates, much less to a *rônin* like Ôishi. He, however, was moved to do so out of courtesy, evidently respecting Ôishi's personality, which he esteemed highly ; but unless he had thought it a matter of grave importance, he would not have taken such special trouble. Ôishi, of course, felt greatly honoured, and at the same time came to think that he must first see this matter out before resorting to the final step. This was one reason why he often appeared to his confederates to be merely procrastinating.

Late in the summer of that year those of the party in Yedo headed by Horibe-Yasubyôye determined on their own account to take speedy action in revenge and wrote repeatedly to Ôishi, pressing him to come up to them. They were so urgent that it seemed that if he did not fall in readily with their wishes, there was every fear of their acting on their own responsibility. Ôishi, who knew the difficulty of the task, was pretty certain that any attempt made without the utmost precautions would be bound to end in failure. And if they once failed, where would he and his party be? No, no rashness now, he thought. The Yedo party must be pacified by all means. One of his leading men, either Yoshida or Hara, must be sent up for that purpose. Hara was then in Osaka with some of the men under him, and so in September Ôishi sent him up with Ushioda-Matanojô and Nakamura-Kansuke. Still Ôishi could not feel quite at ease. As he had, besides, the need of finding out how things were with the enemy, he sent up in October his relative Shindô-Genshirô accompanied by Ôtaka-Gengo.

In the meantime Ôishi was cogitating over the situation he was then in. He had been treated with unusual courtesy by one high in the Government service, who had deigned to write to him, *rônin* as he was, informing him how the case stood. That must not be passed over unacknowledged. He must, if possible, offer his thanks personally. In that case he could avail himself of the opportunity to call on such lords as he knew to ask for their assistance in having his petition granted. Again he could then visit his lord's grave at the Sengakuji Temple and go to pay his respects to the widowed lady, his late mistress. Above all he could then make sure of his party in Yedo, that they would remain united with the others. All things considered, he decided it was best for him to visit Yedo, and so on the 20th of October, accompanied by Okuno-Shôkan, Kawamura-Denbyôye, and Okamura-Jirôzayemon, he started from Kyoto and reached his destination twelve days later.

As soon as he came up to Yedo, Ôishi first of all paid a visit to his lord's grave. Simple as his act was, to him it was weighted with the profoundest emotion. How sad he felt that, though being so near, he could never see his master face to face any more! But as he shut his eyes and bowed in reverence before the tomb, the veil which separated him from his dear lord seemed to dissolve. He felt not only could he see him,—he could even hear him talk, with a strange intimacy at once old and new. Ôishi drank in every word of this master's appeal and smilingly assured him of his best efforts. After some minutes of this spiritual, disembodied communion, he came away consecrated and inspired.

He then went to see the widowed lady. She was at her parents' home, confined in her quiet, simple room, in which was her husband's Buddhist altar, and spending her days lonesomely, dreaming over her happy past or copying out her Sutra. How sweetly surprised she was when Ôishi was announced—Ôishi, about whom of all her old retainers she was wont to talk with the one maid she still employed!

After the first greetings were exchanged, she began with tremulous lips,

" How shall I tell you all I have to say? " and then, borne down by strong emotion, her voice failed her, and murmuring " Pardon me! " feebly, she bowed her face and wept.

Ôishi, moved beyond speech, sat, too, with bent head; and
so for a while the two remained in utter silence, telling each
other in wrapt communion what words could not express.

Then, descending into speech—

" Come near the fire, Kuranosuke ; it's cold, " she said.

" Thank you— "

" I heard you were ill early in the summer. Are you
well now ? "

" Quite well, I thank you. It was only a slight illness,—
nothing worthy of mention. We have been rather anxious
at heart on your account, about your health, your state of
mind. We were sorry that we could not come to see you
so often as we did when our lord was living. I hope you
will take good care of yourself."

" It is kind of you to say so, but, Kuranosuke, . . . "

" Yes ? "

" I wish I were a man. I wish so morning and evening.
A woman's lot is harder to bear than a man's."

" I understand you to the bottom of your soul."

" I am relying only on you. I heard what you did at
Akô and I honoured you with all my heart."

" That was more than I deserved."

" No, it is for me to say so. Our old relation has naturally come to an end, and most of our men have gone away,
Heaven knows where. But, Kuranosuke, I could never
give you up. You are my man as ever."

" I don't know how to thank you for those words of
trust. But my service for three existences has not yet
been finished. Unworthy as I am, I mean to be my lord's
follower even to the other world."

" Ah, your words give me new purpose in life ! I thank

you heartily on my late dear lord's behalf."

Then, telling her maid to bring a purple hood of silken *crêpe*, she said,

" This trifle is my own poor work.   But I shall be very glad if it may serve to wrap you from the winter's cold."

Thanking her, Ôishi looked fondly at his mistress, thinking that it might, indeed, be the last sight he would ever have of her, and slowly, sadly took his leave.

His next business was to call on Araki, Superintendent Officer, to thank him for his sympathy, and this he did accompanied by Okuno.   Then he spent a few days in visiting especially those lords who were related to the Asano family to ask them to use their influence in getting Daigaku appointed heir to his late lord ; so that to all outward appearance he seemed solely bent on the work of restoring his master's house.

But his party in Yedo thought that Ôishi's presence among them was a good opportunity for making arrangements to effect a sudden raid on Kira's mansion and they pressed him for his decision in the matter.   So on the 10th of November, a general meeting was held at Ôishi's lodgings.   Those who met there were fifteen in all, including eight from Kyoto and Osaka.

Then Horibe-Yasubyôye, who was at the head of the Yedo party, began :

" We regret to say that this delay in executing our scheme is tending somewhat to damp our spirits.   We have consulted with Hara, Shindô, and others, whom you kindly sent us, and we have come to the conclusion that to fix a definite time for action is imperative in keeping us braced. In our opinion next March will be the proper time.   We should like to know what our leader says to it."

" I admire your ardour," replied Ôishi. " But I see no need now for fixing the time to attack our enemy. We may do so whenever we get a good opportunity. Only such an opportunity will not come for a while. We have as yet no means of knowing what will become of Sir Daigaku. If we were impatient enough to make an attack on the enemy in spite of that, even if we were successful, we should be blamed for not considering the welfare of our lord's house first of all. To act so would be far from the duty of a faithful retainer. So I say we are not yet ready to fix the time."

Horibe was not to be silenced by this. He said again :

" We understand what you say. But by next March, which will be just a year after the event, Sir Daigaku will be released from confinement and be dealt with in whatever way the Government sees proper. And then, the month being the first anniversary of our lord's death, it is just befitting us to appease his resentment by avenging his wrongs. In any case, unless we fix some definite time for action, we are liable to get demoralized, to an extent I loathe even to imagine. We earnestly desire to have the time fixed for next March."

Ôishi knew that it was rather early, but fearing to depress the ardent spirits of his men, he consented to have it as they desired. The men were overjoyed at his decision. This important point being settled, it was feared that too long a stay in Yedo by their leader would defeat their scheme, so Ôishi, Hara, and others soon left for their separate homes in the west.

What effect had Ôishi's public appearance in Yedo on

Kira and his side ? Kira had been relieved of his official
duties and was now leading a retired life at Matsuzaka-chô,
Honjô, on the other side of the River Sumida, where he
had been ordered to move early in September from near
Gofukubashi.   This, by the way, gave great convenience
to the Akô party, for his former residence being just
inside the castle moat, an attack on it would have constituted
a trespass on the castle grounds.   So many men said, after
the famous raid had been accomplished, that this change of
residence was really an act of Providence in favour of the
loyalists.   Now Ôishi's staying in Yedo was ostensibly for
advancing the cause of restoring the house of Asano, but
it did not fail to impress the enemy with the idea that Ôishi
was far from retiring from active life and that in spite of
his settling at Yamashina, he would not rest till his end was
gained one way or another.   A dangerous person he still
seemed to Kira, and Chisaka, councillor to Lord Uesugi,
redoubled his endeavours to guard Kira from harm and
sent spy after spy to Kyoto to watch every movement of
Ôishi.

But before examining Ôishi's bold strategem to outwit
his enemy, we must describe what happend in the next two
months at Yamashina, for it was a sort of crisis in the history
of the secret league of the Akô men.   It was now January
of the fifteenth year of Genroku (1702), and in Ôishi's
mind two wishes kept coming and going : he wanted to
take revenge and at the same time to get the house of Asano
restored.   So while preparing for the one, he was at great
pains to bring the other plan to fruition.   This was
inevitably so with the man who had been the chief pillar
of the clan and was still so in a sense, though that clan had

gone to pieces never to rise again of its own will. This state of Ôishi's mind was easily legible to the other ex-retainers, so that not only those who were loyal to the bone but even those more opportunist in mind sent in written pledges, and the number of the league members increased steadily.

The report that Kira had retired from the headship of the family in the middle of the previous month and was succeeded by his son reached Ôishi's men in the Kyoto district, and with it came the rumour that before long Kira himself would be invited to live in Yonezawa, the fief of Lord Uesugi. As this would bar for good any assault on him, the Akô men were very much excited, and the most radical among them, headed by Hara and Ôtaka and urged on by the Yedo party, pressed Ôishi to carry out what had been agreed upon in Yedo. That was, however, only a tentative idea with Ôishi, and he thought it was still premature to take up arms. He again felt the need of pacifying the Yedo men and wished to send up to them one who was so able as to act in his stead. And that was no other than Yoshida-Chûzayemon who was second only to Ôishi in leadership. Yoshida willingly acceded to his request provided that the men in the Kyoto district would come to some agreement of opinion so that he could act on the strength of it. This Ôishi thought reasonable and summoned his men to Kyoto.

For several days, beginning with the 15th of February, meetings were secretly held. But it was extremely hard for the men to arrive at an agreement. This was as might be expected, for there were three groups among them, one being the moderates—and they formed the majority—who

with Ôishi desired both to have the house of Asano restored
and to take revenge on their late master's behalf; a second,
the opportunists, by no means small in number, who
behind a screen of loyal talk were thinking only of their
own interests with an eye to the time when by Ôishi's
efforts the house of Asano should be restored; and a third,
the radicals, who were all for immediate vengeance.   Under
such circumstances, it was but natural that there should be
great divergence of opinion.

The last meeting was held at Yamashina, and the air of
the room was full of tension.   The moderates were waiting
for Ôishi to speak and the opportunists were watching
developments in silence.   So it was the radicals who opened
the discussion.

"There was no sign of change," said one of them to
Ôishi, "in our enemy's movements until we had our
conference in Yedo last November.   But even then you
agreed to have the time for our assault fixed for next month.
Now that Kira has gone into retirement and may, as is
rumoured, be taken over to Yonezawa at any time, we must
be all the more prompt in action.   How is it then that you
are still hesitating to make up your mind?"

"I cannot blame you for being puzzled at my intentions,"
replied Ôishi, "but as I said repeatedly at the Yedo conference, we must first see what will become of Sir Daigaku.
If by good fortune he be appointed heir to our late lord,
even in the capacity of a petty daimyô, it would save the
honour of our master to some extent.   I don't think it
the proper duty of his surviving followers to hasten rashly
into action without giving that due consideration.   I
merely approved the opinion of the Yedo men as a

temporary expedient, fearing that their spirits might be depressed by too much opposition. The time has not yet come. I can approve no rashness."

The radicals grew all the more excited at these words.

" Suppose we wait till Sir Daigaku is appointed heir to our late lord. Then if we make a raid on Kira's mansion after that, will it not bring down ruin again upon our lord's house, which we have taken so much pains to have restored? Do you intend, then, to give up our revenge altogether if the house is restored? "

Ôishi shook his head.

" No ; restoration is restoration and revenge is revenge. The two things must not be confounded. It is true we must not attack Kira in force supposing our lord's house is restored. But the sworn enemy of our lord cannot be left untouched. If our first object is attained, I will be avenged on Kira alone on behalf of you all."

But Hara would not hear of this.

" Not only," said he, " we who have remained true to the pledge since last March, but also those who have joined us from time to time, have all one thing in view, and will not swerve from our resolution, which is to take revenge. But if you acted, as you say, as our sole repre-sentative, where would the rest of us be? We should be derided as cowards totally unworthy of the name of samurai. As we hate the thought of being called so, we want to carry out our scheme at once. Our lord was lord of all the Akô men ; he was a lord to you and a lord to all the rest of us here. One should not live under the same sky with the slayer of one's lord or father, as the saying is. I know not what others may think of the matter, but for my part give me a chance for immediate attack or instant death."

Ôtaka-Gengo, Ushioda-Matanojô, and Nakamura-Kan-suke at once agreed.

"What Hara says is very true. We cannot stay our hands till we have imbrued our swords in our enemy's blood."

Loud cries of assent rose on all sides, and the party seemed to be about to split.

Yoshida-Chûzayemon and Onodera-Jûnai, two elder members of the league, who had been listening to the discussion thoughtfully, now expressed their concurrent opinion.

"We do not think that Master Ôishi means to say that he alone is going to play the part of a loyal samurai. He is only anxious that your ardour shall not hinder the restoration of our lord's affairs. At the same time he had no mind to lessen the effect of your loyalty. We hope that you will not take his words in ill part. Nevertheless we admire your zeal as something rarely met with in the world. To tell the truth, we old fellows, too, are hoping to have a dig at the enemy before finishing our short journey to the grave . . . "

They ended by indirectly urging Ôishi to reconsider his decision. On this the leader said :

"I feel deeply moved to see you all as faithful as ever and I assure you I will share your fortunes with you. Only we must first wait to see the outcome of our petition. By next month, as it is the anniversary of our late lord's death, we hope we may hear from the Government about the matter. If not, we must wait another year. If we are not honoured with a gracious decision even then, our hope will be lost for ever. And no way will be left to us but to attack our enemy in a body and satisfy our lord's resentment by cutting off his head.   So I desire you all to agree with me and trust me to fix the course of our united action."

This was the most critical moment for the loyal league, and but for Ôishi's moral influence and sincerity, it would scarcely have escaped a fatal schism.   But hearing his open-hearted avowal, even the radicals could not turn against him.

" If you, Master Ôishi, assure us of a final attack sooner or later, we will submit to your discretion in the matter and abide our time."

So they said, and all came to that agreement.

" Then let us renew our pledge," proposed Ôishi ; and all those present pledged themselves again with seals of blood.   And on the 21st of February Yoshida hastened to Yedo with the resolution passed at Yamashina.

Henceforth Yoshida stayed in Yedo communicating with Yamashina and Hara in Osaka communicating with both Yamashina and Akô, while Ôishi in his headquarters at Yamashina with Onodera as the chief of the staff controlled the whole party, defraying the party expenses out of the reserve funds he had kept for the restoration of the house of Asano.   Thus their battle array being perfected, they only waited for their hour to strike.

Now Kira, though gone into retirement, was by no means entirely at his ease : he was always under the impression that he might be attacked at any moment.   Indeed, his old wife from the Uesugi family had been bold enough to advise him to commit *seppuku* as a samurai should before suffering disgrace at the hands of his enemies, but he was too cowardly to have the heart for such an act and was only seeking refuge under the shell of vigilance like a fish. He was, indeed, aided by Chisaka, wise councillor of Lord Uesugi, as has been already said. But Chisaka was a very prudent man and would not take the responsibility of bringing Kira either to Uesugi's castle in Yonézawa or to his villa at Azabu, Yedo, for though that would secure Kira from any attack of the Akô men, he would have been acting against his usual principle of discretion and keeping out of harm's way. It was Chisaka's bounden duty to protect the house of Uesugi at any cost, and he acted accordingly not only in this case but also later at the time when he received the report of the raid made on Kira's mansion ; he then stopped Lord Uesugi at the risk of his own life, from going to his father's mansion to fight with the raiders. In employing spies he was also wary enough to instruct them never to be offensive, so that they might not irritate the enemy to rash action. Indeed, he was even wishing that the house of Asano might be restored, for he thought that evil would then be averted without useless bloodshed. So, except for the strongly guarded state of Kira's mansion, the Akô *rônin* were not very much troubled by the support given him by Lord Uesugi. But the spies were something of a nuisance, while they did much to keep Kira on the alert. And these Ôishi now undertook to throw completely off the scent.

It was much against his secret inclination that Ôishi now turned to vicious pleasures, but as a dissolute life is often the last resort of those who seek to drown sorrow, shame or disappointment in debauchery and drink, so he now began to indulge in dissipation to pretend that he had given up in despair all ideas of revenge.   In judging his conduct, we must, of course, take into consideration the peculiarity of the time he lived in, called the Genroku period, when in consequence of amassing wealth and prosperity, people had grown luxurious and indolent, and pleasure-seeking was looked upon as a mere indication of fashionable living. Still to indulge in it as Ôishi did was carrying extravagance a little too far.   The famous red-light quarters in the Kyoto district in those days were Shimabara, Gion, and Fushimi, and he nightly frequented those places by turns and even went occasionally as far as Nara and Osaka. *Rônin* as he was, he had been the chief retainer of Akô and seemed to have an inexhaustible supply of money, which he spent with lavish liberality, often scattering handfuls of silver like rain to the extreme delight of his entertainers. Soon he was known by the name of Uki-sama and was made much of in those quarters of the three cities.   His real intention being known to his confederates, they mostly accompanied their chief to such places and vied with him in showing to the world how dissolute they, too, had grown in their despair.

These houses of pleasure having a sort of extraterritorial status, they were very convenient for secret consultations, and so while youthful members of the league pretended that they had given themselves up utterly to debauchery, their leaders conferred from time to time and matured their plans.   But the main object of these scenes of wild debauchery was to advertise to the world the depraved level to which the gang had sunk and so under the influence of *saké*, Ôishi and his companions, accompanied by many geisha-girls and jesters, would sometimes appear in Gion

Park or such public places and in full view of Kyoto people
indulge in unrestrained carousals, casting all decency to
the winds and shocking sober-minded folk.   So before
long especially Ôishi's profligacy exposed him to the
abuse of the world, and he came to be looked down on as
a hopeless samurai, who had renounced all idea of taking
revenge for his lord.   And the spies, witnessing his miserable plight, decided there was nothing more to fear from him
and began to withdraw to Yedo.

It was now summer.   The anniversary of Lord Asano
had come round a month or so before, but no news of
Daigaku being released from confinement came to Ôishi.
He felt uneasy and feared for the worst.   After deliberating
deeply, he made up his mind to start preparing for action
first by freeing himself from all encumbrances.   He had
a happy, peaceful home with a wise good woman for his
wife and a family of four healthy children.   But he must
sacrifice them for the great cause ; the path of duty is ever
steep and thorny.

One day he called his son Chikara to his room and said :

"As you are fifteen years old and are coming of age
pretty soon, I hope you will understand what I tell you now.
In the conduct of life nothing is greater than duty, but it is
supreme only in the relation of a vassal to his lord.   As
you know, I owe great obligations to my late lord and am
going to repay them with my life.   You were too young to
receive any fief from him, but it is all due to him that you
have grown so big, fed and clothed with what he gave to
me.   Have you a mind to walk with me in the path of duty ?
I could not find it in my heart to invite my son to death.
But we must all die sooner or later.   How much better is

it then to die now honourably than to live on in dishonour and die an ignominious death ? It is from my deep love for you that I want you to choose the noble course. But if you don't understand me, I have no more to say ; you need not follow your father. I am going to divorce your mother and send her away with her children to her old home in Toyoöka. You may go with her if you like. Now, think well and give me your answer."

Chikara, wiping his tears away, looked up reproachfully into his father's face.

" Why are you in doubt about my mind ? I have come to know something of duty through your instruction. How can I leave my father, turn my back on our lord, and disgrace myself ? Let me die with you, father, I pray, and be it known that father and son have followed their lord in death."

" Well said, Chikara. You are my son.—Well, I'll tell you how good our late lord was to you. One day soon after you were born, he came to visit our home. And seeing you growing healthy, he was pleased to give you a beautiful sword for self-protection. And then I think you remember that when I took you at the age of four or five years to the castle to present you to him, he called you to his side and asked what you liked best. When you answered that you best liked a pony, he called you a brave child and selected for you a fine one from his stable. Was he not a kind lord to you ?"

Chikara nodded smiling and felt all the more the responsibility of a noble task laid on his shoulders. Then Ôishi let him call his wife to him. He told her how the matter stood and gave her a letter of divorce. He did this out of pity that his wife and children might not suffer from his act, for according to the law in those days, for any serious crime not only the offender himself but also his family were punished.   Be that as it might, it was heart-rending for Ôishi to have to separate from wife and children, never to meet one another again till life was over.

After he had settled these things about his home, Ôishi grew more dissolute than ever.   He did so to conceal his real intention, by making the world believe that he had no thoughts beyond his pleasures and that he had driven away his wife and children to be able to indulge in them still more freely.   But this worked so well that many even of his confederates began to doubt his true intentions and grow tired of him.   Koyama and Shindô, relatives of Ôishi, agreed that it must be partly due to his having no partner at home and that they would recommend him a mistress to make him less profligate.   They were two of those who, with many others, finally went back on their pledge and left the league, and it was thought by some that taking advantage of his weakness, they schemed to turn his mind away from his original intention by making him infatuated with a woman.   At any rate they selected a girl named O-Karu, noted throughout Kyoto for her beauty and succeeded in getting him to take her for his mistress. Ôishi loved her extremely but contrary to expectation, he never desisted from frequenting the gay quarters and wallowing in low pleasures.   Even the few spies who were still sneaking about thought it waste of time to watch him any longer, and nearly all had left the Kyoto district by the end of summer.

On July 22nd a special messenger sent by Yoshida in

Yedo arrived at Yamashina, bringing a report of great importance, to the effect that Daigaku was released from confinement at last but had been placed in the custody of Asano-Akinokami in his province without having his fief restored to him. Daigaku was thus condemned to exile for his brother's crime and his name was cancelled from the official book of heraldry, not to be resuscitated. Ôishi was swept by a great wave of deep emotion. All his hopes to secure the restoration of his lord's house, for which he had worked and waited for more than a year, were dashed to earth : his endeavours were in vain. One way only now remained to him and he rose resolutely to embrace it.

Prior to this the more radical members of the league both in Yedo and in the Kyoto district had grown impatient again to carry out their intention. They were disgusted with the way in which Ôishi was procrastinating and thought that by taking a resolute step by themselves, they could appease their late lord's spirit without forcing Ôishi to compromise. So they collected a dozen or so willing men and agreed to start to Yedo in twos and threes by the 26th of July. On the previous day, however, the report of the final disposition of Daigaku's case reached Horibe, who was then in Kyoto for the purpose of inducing his friends to take immediate action. By so narrow a margin had the party escaped from disruption, for Horibe saw at once the needlessness of keeping his plan secret and went to see Ôishi who, as we have seen, was ready for the final step. And so they agreed to hold a secret conference for making all necessary arrangements to that end on the 28th, at Maruyama in Kyoto.

The conference did not last long, nor was there now any

heated discussion in it, for all those present were of one mind, glad to be nearing at last their long-wished-for hour. Only Ôishi laid stress on taking the utmost precautions to ensure success.   He said that as he had several things to attend to before starting, he would go up to Yedo by October and so hoped that everyone would manage to be there before him.   He desired that they would feel out the enemy as much as they could, but refrain from stealing a march on the others.   His instructions should be strictly followed for the honour of the league they had formed. The joy of those assembled was unbounded and they could not but celebrate the day by drinking success to one another.

Ôishi set about at once to make his preparations.   He ordered from a certain merchant in Kyoto the upper garments to be worn by the loyalists in the attack.   They were firemen's dark mantles with hoods, which were quite appropriate for a night attack, for they would make the movements of the men less conspicuous while at the same time protecting them from the inclemency of bad weather.   As to weapons, as Lord Asano had been a collector of fine swords, Ôishi had been able to put aside plenty of them out of the store at Akô.   Other weapons such as spears and bows and arrows, as well as mallets and ladders, could be easily had in Yedo.   But there was one thing which troubled Ôishi most and that was the weeding-out of doubtful members of the league.

The membership, which had steadily increased since the spring, now reached 12 in number, excluding 4 who had died.   The league looked on the surface flourishing, but as a number of members had other ulterior objects in joining it, they became crest-fallen on hearing of the failure of their hopes concerning Daigaku, while even such men as Okuno, Shindô, and Koyama, who had been Ôishi's confidants from the first, began to assume an ambigious attitude. Ôishi thought that he could place no dependence on such broken reeds, but as he had their written promises with him, he could not dismiss them off-hand. So he thought of a plan of discarding them by returning them their papers, so that he would have nothing more to do with them while yet keeping them in countenance, however mean their conduct might be. For this purpose he selected Kaiga-Yazayemon and Ôtaka-Gengo, men of easy address, and sent them out to call on many of the members.

Ôishi's plan took, and though in fine the number of firm members was reduced to less than half what it had been originally, Ôishi was glad to make sure of them, and felt convinced that he could now carry out with the rest what he had intended from the first in accordance with the spirit of the samurai, to whom life or death was indifferent and duty the sole object in life. By the end of September nearly all the staunch loyalists who stood by Ôishi went up to Yedo, parting for ever from their parents or wives and children. And so disposing of his property and raising what little sum he could, the funds for the party expenses running short by that time, Ôishi under a feigned name started from an inn in Kyoto, on the 7th of October, accompanied by five of his confederates. Like a general marching with his army, he now proudly brought up the rear, picturing to himself the decisive battle in which he was going to engage and feeling sure of the ultimate victory that would crown his zealous efforts.

RETRIBUTION AT LAST!

Ôishi arrived at Kamakura on the 21st of October, where he was met by Yoshida and Tominomori, and stayed there for three days. Then, instead of going straight to Yedo, he went to a retreat near Kawasaki, arranged for him by Tominomori the previous year. His progress was wariness itself. He sojourned there for about ten days, feeling out the state of things in the city, and finding it apparently pretty safe to be there, he joined his son Chikara, who had come up before him, at a hotel in Nihombashi.

Now about sixty of the Akô men, inclusive of servants, were in Yedo, lodging in various inns or living in their own humble homes, all having assumed feigned names as well as occupations. It might be wondered how they escaped suspicion in that well-ordered city, however careful they might be in their movements. Indeed, it soon began to be rumoured about that many Akô *rônin* had found their way into Yedo and were on Kira's track so that there was really no reason why the authorities should remain ignorant of the fact. The truth was, however, that though the matter was already known to them, they were of opinion that, since the Akô men seemed to have no intention of defying the laws but were only trying to do their duty as faithful followers by appeasing the resentful spirit of their deceased master, they might well be let alone, out of a feeling of knightly sympathy unless or until they actually took up arms. Fortunate indeed they were that this was so, for so they were enabled to proceed with their work without any impediment except what might be offered by the enemy.

As soon as Ôishi arrived at his hotel, he called together Yoshida and Hara, the assistant leaders, and Onodera, the chief of the staff, and heard their reports.   They agreed to divide the younger members into four groups and let them go scouting every night by turns to examine the defences of Kira's mansion and his movements and whereabouts. Receiving these orders, they disguised themselves as servants, tradesmen, and such like, loitered about the neighbourhood of the enemy's house till daybreak, and reported everything they saw or heard.   The matter, however, was not left to them alone.   One of the elders, such as Yoshida, joined them almost every night and examining every broad and narrow street in the neighbourhood, thought out the best ways of meeting Uesugi's men in case they should come up to help, so that a handful of men might stand against heavy odds till their main object was attained.   The Akô men were on their own guard too. As Uesugi's men were noted for bravery, it was feared that Ôishi might be assaulted at any moment.   So every precaution was taken against such an emergency, for if their leader had met with any disaster, it would have not only brought disgrace to the party but also led to the failure of their attempt, which was more than they could bear to contemplate.

Time passed quickly and they were now in December. If only Kira's whereabouts had been definitely known, they could have made a raid at any time.   So on the 2nd Ôishi summoned all the members to a restaurant in Fukagawa under the pretence of forming a sort of club for pooling their finances.   It was in fact to renew their mutual vows, (for some few cases of defection had occurred even after the members assembled in Yedo), and to make them throughly informed of the part each one should play in the attack.   In the written pledge prepared for the occasion, stress was laid on three points : first, that it should be deemed there was no difference in honour or merit between the various parts, which each one was assigned to play ; secondly, that all should act in the spirit of mutual help regardless of personal feelings ; and thirdly, that they should not feel free to act as they wished even after Kira was killed.   The pledge was read aloud by Hara, and amid grave silence everyone put his name on the paper, sealing with his blood.

Forty-seven names were counted, the names of all who were present that day.   There had been fifty-five members in the previous month ; by the end of the month five of them had dropped away, and now in two days three more had left the league for ever !

Presently Ôishi took up a note of detailed instructions and called everyone's attention to them.   They dealt with

1)   the places where they were to assemble on the appointed day ;

2)   punctuality ;

3)   the treatment of the enemy's head, when obtained ;

4)   the blowing of whistles as signals of success ;

5)   the treatment of wounded comrades ;

6)   the beating of a gong as a signal of retreat ;

7)   the way out and the places where they were to withdraw

        guarding against counter-attacks ;

9)   how to deal with official and other interventions, and so forth, making in all thirteen items.   The men all

noted them carefully and felt that the time was, indeed, drawing near for dealing a blow once for all. And at dusk, hearing the plovers crying in the offing, they dispersed : priests, physicians, masters, and tradesmen, all peaceful-looking sorts of men !

In the meantime a valuable thing came into the hands of the leaders. This was nothing less than a plan of Kira's mansion, so eagerly sought after to ensure success. But as it happened to be an old one, painstaking efforts were taken to find out what alterations, if any, had been made in the building till they became sure of the position of Kira's room as well as his son's. In this Kanzaki-Yogorô, disguised as a rice dealer, showed his excellent detective skill.

Another clever detective was Ôtaka-Gengo, who, disguising himself as a rich dealer in drapery of Kyoto, went to take lessons in the tea ceremoney under a certain master who was also Kira's. He happened to find out that there would be a ceremonial tea party at Kira's on the morning of the 6th of December. The news was, indeed, a piece of good luck, for what the Akô men wanted to get day and night was a positive proof that Kira would be in his house on such and such a day. So it was settled for the nonce to attack him on the night of the 5th, and they endeavoured to get further information to corroborate that report. Then it transpired that the tea party at Kira's on the 6th was suddenly postponed on account of the Shogun's going to visit the mansion of Lord Matsudaira on the previous day. They were greatly disappointed, but as there was no help for it, they looked for another chance. About a week had passed without any more news, when a report

came again from Ôtaka that a year-end tea party would be
held at Kira's on the evening of the 14th, with Lord Ôtomo
as an honoured guest.   The 14th!—was it not the very
death-day of Lord Asano? How strange and at the same
time how ominous! Ôishi in receiving the report felt at
once that success was in his grasp.   As luck would have it,
the report was confirmed again and again ; indeed, in one
case Yokokawa-Kampei, one of the confederates, was by
good chance asked by a priest of his acquaintance, who was
also invited, to take his letter of acceptance to Kira.   There
was no doubt about it, and it was declared, though secretly,
that the attack would be made on the night of the 14th to
a dead certainty.

The snow which had begun to fall on the 11th continued
till the 14th, so that the city of Yedo was buried deep
beneath it, presenting a sea of soft, silvery undulation
and even human voices were hushed as if covered with
a heavy blanket.   In such quietness, the Akô men made
preparations for the day, speedily and yet noiselessly, for
it was agreed that everything had to be ready by the evening.
But those who could manage went with Ôishi to the
Sengakuji Temple at Takanawa to pay their farewell homage
to the grave of Lord Asano there.

Getting a room in the temple to themselves, Ôishi gave
them his final instructions.   He was going, he said, to
divide his men into two companies.   He would lead one
company himself and make a raid on Kira's mansion from
the east or front gate, while his son Chikara, on the recommendation of the staff, would take the other company and
force his way in from the west or rear gate.   As his son was
still a boy, he would be assisted by two elder leaders,

Yoshida and Onodera ; the three should act as one. The
only man they were aiming at was Kira, so time must not
be wasted in fighting with any others. They must join
together to make quick work of it. Only those who
offered resistance were to be disabled, no others. The
fighting indoors had to be done by the younger members,
and the older ones were to stay outside, cutting off the
enemy's retreat and guarding against any interference.
The passwords in the darkness would be " *Yama* (moun-
tain) " and " *Kawa* (river) " and those who were not ready
with them were to be treated as enemies.   And if perchance
they should fail to attain their object, they were to set fire
to the house and all to commit *seppuku* on the spot. By
two o'clock that night, they were to assemble at the three
places already chosen for the purpose. He finished his
speech by asking those present to inform their comrades of
all this.   With so much care Ôishi as chief leader instruct-
ed his men and they felt that nothing now remained to be
done but to wait for the night.

The three trysting places chosen were all in the same ward
as Kira's mansion : one was Horibe-Yasubyôye's and another was Sugino-Jûheiji's, both of which were convenient
for many people to assemble, for the two had given themselves out to be fencing masters.   A third was Kanzaki's
rice shop which was most near to Kira's mansion. All
the weapons and accoutrements except the swords which
were already in the hands of the men, had been stored
at Horibe's to be distributed at any time. And by two
o'clock all were at their assigned places ready to form up
into companies.

Let us now glance at the age of the forty-seven loyalists,

who may be arranged as follows :—

Horibe-Yahyôye	aged	76,	Akabane-Genzô	aged	34,
Hazama-Kihyôye	,,	68,	Horibe-Yasubyôye	,,	33,
Yoshida-Chûzayemon	,,	62,	Fuwa-Kazuyemon	,,	33,
Mase-Kyûdaiyû	,,	62,	Chikamatsu-Kanroku	,,	33,
Muramatsu-Kihyôye	,,	61,	Tominomori-Sukeyemon	,,	33,
Onodera-Jûnai	,,	60,	Kurahashi-Densuke	,,	33,
Okuda-Magodayû	,,	56,	Takebayashi-Tadashichi	,,	32,
Hara-Sôyemon	,,	55,	Ôtaka-Gengo	,,	31,
Kaiga-Yazayemon	,,	53,	Yoshida-Sawayemon	,,	28,
Chiba-Saburôbyôye	,,	50,	Yada-Gorôyemon	,,	28,
Kimura-Okayemon	,,	45,	Onodera-Kôyemon	,,	27,
Ôishi-Kuranosuke	,,	44,	Sugino-Jûheiji	,,	27,
Nakamura-Kansuke	,,	44,	Ôishi-Sezayemon	,,	26,
Suganoya-Hannojô	,,	43,	Muramatsu-Sandayû	,,	26,
Hayami-Tôzayemon	,,	39,	Okuda-Sadayemon	,,	25,
Maebara-I uke	,,	39,	Hazama-Jûjirô	,,	25,
Terasaka-Kichiyemon	,,	38,	Isogai-Jûrôzayemon	,,	24,
Okajima-Yasoyemon	,,	37,	Okano-Kinyemon	,,	23,
Kanzaki-Yogorô	,,	37,	Hazama-Shinroku	,,	23,
Kayano-Wasuke	,,	36,	Katsuta-Shinzayemon	,,	23,
Kataoka-Gengoyemon	,,	36,	Mase-Magokurô	,,	22,
Yokogawa-Kampei	,,	36,	Yatô-Yemonshichi	,,	17,
Mimura-Jirôzayemon	,,	36,	Ôishi-Chikara	,,	15.
Ushioda-Matanojô	,,	34,			

We find here that one was over seventy, five were in their sixties, four in their fifties and forties, eighteen in their thirties, thirteen in their twenties, and two in their teens. Disparity in years seemed to make no difference to these men, whose strength lay not so much in their arms as in their prowess and spirit for upholding the cause of justice. The existence of two youngsters under twenty among them is especially noteworthy, showing how zeal made men of them. As might be expected, the backbone of the party, however, was formed by men in their thirties, who were eighteen in number, while the ruling spirits such as Ôishi, Yoshida, Hara, and Onodera were all just at that ripe age of over forty.

As the appointed hour drew near, the Akô men assembled at the three trysting-places already mentioned and began to dress themselves. They used everything new from under-clothes to upper garment. Purity in clothing is an important prerequisite with Japanese in undertaking anything special under divine protection, and they, of course, believed that their deed would be acceptable in the sight of Heaven. Their underwear was all of wadded *habutae*-silk, soft and smooth to the skin. Over that each put on a coat of mail covered with satin or damask. Then a wadded black silk garment crested and lined with red or pink thin silk was donned. With trouser-like *hakama* over mailed drawers besides gauntlets and leggings, their attire was complete. A mantle and hood of broadcloth for outdoor wear remained to be put on.

How luxurious, we may think, their costume was for the mere purpose of fighting! For this we must partly take into consideration the taste of the period they were in, when everything was for splendour and showiness. But the real significance of the unusual care they took in dressing lay in their anxiety to guard against any misunderstanding they might incur of having been driven to this deed of deadly bloodshed by mere desperation at their poverty,—and it was true that most of the loyalists, indeed, were hard up by that time—and also to lead people to the right recognition of their true motive, which was so sacred to them that in nothing short of immaculateness could they dare follow it. And indeed, they went so far as to burn incense in their hoods so that even death might not cast defilement at once over their remains.

Having finished dressing, all were ready to go. They took now a simple parting drink and the men at the first and second meeting places assembled at the third, which was Kanzaki's shop. A temple bell was heard striking four : it was the signal for starting and headed by Kanzaki, who was followed by a man holding up a pole on which was fastened a box containing a statement of the retainers of Asano-Takuminokami, the whole party carrying each a spear, a halberd, a bow and arrows, a mallet, or a bamboo ladder, marched on in silence, a long line of black figures without lantern or torch. But the snow was crisp under foot and made walking easy. And a morning moon now shining bright, the whole snowy scene was all the more silvery and distinctly visible as if in daylight. They felt that they were guided by the spirit of their late lord, and their blood tingled at the thought. Approaching Kira's mansion, they stopped and parted in two, one company making for the front gate and the other for the rear.

Now Kira's house was, of course, closely guarded. Not only had Kira himself many swordsmen in his service, but also Uesugi had sent him many of his retainers for assistance. These men lived in tenement-houses on the premises, ready for any emergency. But Kira had come to make light of his chief enemy ever since he had been deceived by the latter's stratagems, and thought that though possibly some others among the Akô men might still be hoping to carry out their vengeance, he need fear nothing worse than a road attack by three or five of them at most. He was, indeed, deluded by this sense of security. Little

dreaming that the loyalists were assembled in his neighbourhood and were waiting for the hour of attack, he was
enjoying a good time with Lord Ôtomo, his old colleague,
till very late.   And now, tired out after the entertainment,
everyone in the house was sound asleep.

The east gate, being the main one, was very strongly
built, and it was not the intention of the men there to try
to break it open.   Two ladders were put up against it, and
soon the company of twenty-three assailants had scaled it
and were down on the other side.   The rear gate needed
no such trouble; it yielded easily to the blows of their
mallets and the twenty-four assembled there were soon
inside.   They could and would no longer hold back : no
thought of retreat was theirs.   They had hoped for this for
more than eighteen months.   Now they had but to find
Kira and kill him before the dawn ; it was the demand of
the age and people as well.   Their honour was more precious to them than their lives.   They must at all hazards
attain their object.

The men broke down doors and struggled to force
their way in.   Ôishi with Hara and Mase stayed quietly
outside, guarding against possible interference.   Hara
especially felt mad with impatience to go inside and join
the younger men, but seeing Ôishi so patient and sedate
he could not ask his permission to do so.

Following the harsh noise of breaking doors came the
noise of sliding-screens crashing, and the loud shouts of
men ; then suddenly the clash of swords and a dying cry.

" Somebody done for ? " queried Ôishi coolly.

" Sounds like it : one of the enemy, I think."

" I hope so."

Again rose louder the shouts of men, the crash of sliding-screens, the shrieks of women and children, and the clash of swords. If was more terrible to listen in inaction to the struggle than to fight. The three men strained their ears to catch the sound of the whistle, which should be the signal that Kira was found.

But that eagerly awaited sound took long in coming. The noise of panels breaking, the shrieks, the clash of swords grew louder and then fainter like waves rolling in and receding. Shouts like those of the Akô men were heard unceasingly. They seemed to be fighting with desperate courage. Flying forms appeared at times, seeking to break through from the inferno within, but their escape was cut off by those stationed outside. The Akô men seemed to be winning.

The neighbouring people were now up and there were crowds gathered outside the front gate. Inside the noise subsided in a general way, but no whistling was heard as yet.

" What's the matter ? " asked Hara.

" Wait and we shall hear," responded his leader.

" May I go in and see how things are going ? "

" If you do not take long."

Hara went in but soon came back.

" Kira is not yet found. But as search is being made everywhere, he cannot long elude us."

" How is the fight progressing ? "

" Oh, it is awful. Corpses are thick everywhere. But they are all of the enemy and none of our side have been killed. All are in high spirits."

" It takes long to find Kira ? "

" Yes ; he is hiding somewhere. But there's no way for him to escape."

Time was passing quickly. In the uncanny quietness, even Ôishi grew impatient and prayed almost unconsciously, " O Spirit of Lord Asano, help us now ! " But no whistle came as yet to their ears.

" Then, is all up with us ? Have all our efforts come to nothing ? Must we now kill ourselves as the last step ? "

Every leader was asking so in his mind. And they could not help seeing that dawn was beginning to whiten the sky.

But it was just at that moment that they heard shouts of a few men and a shriek. " What ? " they asked, but again all turned quiet.

" Lost, then," muttered Hara to himself.

Suddenly the shrill sound of a whistle broke the silence and it was answered and repeated here and there.

" Heavens ! " the three cried and all ran in.

When Ôishi and the others reached the room whence the sound of whistles came, nearly all the men were assembled. It was noisy with the clamour of voices shouting confusedly, their words hardly distinguishable. In the centre an old man lay at his last gasp. He was Kira, found at last in a fuel-shed near the kitchen and dragged out there to await Ôishi's inspection. A white silk sleeping-robe, half torn from his shoulders, exposed to the light of the candles a scar, the sign of a sword cut now healed.

Yoshida said to Ôishi in a voice shaken with unrestrained emotion,

" Look here ! This is the cut given by our lord."

" No doubt about it," Ôishi said and prostrated himself

before the old man. It was to worship the wound, and he wept for the first time in his life.

Ôishi now stood up and gave the old man his quietus. And finding that Hazama had brought Kira down, he let him cut the head off the corpse. A great shout of triumph was sent up three times, the shout expressing everything dear to the loyal hearts of the Akô men.

Presently, the gong being struck, the men assembled at the rear gate. When the roll was called, no one was found missing—forty-seven men as before, among whom three had got some bruises and only one a slight sword-cut. After seeing that the house was secure from fire, they marched out with the head of Kira wrapped in his sleeve and held high on a spear.

They stayed for a while in front of the Ekôin Temple just near by, ready to meet the reinforcements from the house of Uesugi, which they expected every moment; but as no enemy came in sight, Ôishi ordered them to withdraw to the Sengakuji Temple. A procession was formed. As the vanguard two men with spears went first; then a man holding Kira's head high on his spear and guarded by several men followed. Ôishi-Kuranosuke came next, walking in dignity alone, with all the rest following after. As it was the fifteenth, the day for daimyô to go to the castle for their monthly attendance, the route was so chosen that they might expose themselves as little as possible to public gaze. Still in passing some daimyô's mansions, they were challenged once or twice, but they managed to reach Asano's family temple at Takanawa.

There they held before the tomb of Lord Asano a ceremony to report their deed to his spirit, a ceremony most

solemn and impressive to the loyal men. Kira's head,
cleansed of blood, was offered to the tomb on a stand,
before which burning incense rose from a censer in thin
cloudlets of sweet perfume. From lines of the loyalists
kneeling in the snow, Ôishi advanced a few steps towards
the grave and offering some incense, made a low bow.
Taking a dirk out of his breast and unsheathing it, he laid
it on a stone step with the handle towards the grave and
the blade towards the head. This was meant to imply
that his lord might now satisfy his long-endured resentment himself. Then he receded a step or two and knelt
again, bowing long. While he was doing this silently, he
was apologizing for his vain efforts to have the house of
his lord restored and reporting on behalf of his men what
had been done with their lives that morning to pay back,
though it was only an infinitesimal part, the debt of obligations they owed him. All felt this and bowed with Ôishi
till they were moved to silent tears. Then Ôishi stood up
and taking the dirk, struck Kira's head three times with
it in his lord's stead. When all was done, he burned incense in his personal capacity and let his men follow
his example. By unanimous consent, Hazama-Jûjirô, who
had been the first to stab Kira, took the lead ; then followed
Takebayashi-Tadashichi who had given Kira a cut, and so
on till everyone there had performed the rite.

The men then went into the temple and taking a rest, a-
waited the orders of the Government. At this point there
is one thing to be mentioned. And this is the mysterious
disappearance of one member, Terasaka-Kichiyemon by
name, who stood lowest among the retainers. The truth
was that Ôishi secretly sent him as a messenger to Asano's

widowed lady to report the success of the attack, for of all
persons in the world it was she whom Ôishi thought it his
most pleasant duty to inform of it as soon as possible.
Moreover, in the parcel containing the letter of report was
an account book in which all the party expenses he had
defrayed out of the ten thousand *ryô* in his keeping were
entered, a small residue in cash being placed within the
cover. It was just one more small instance of Ôishi's
integrity. We may well imagine how deeply touched the
lady felt by it.

To return; prior to the arrival of the triumphal procession at the temple, Ôishi sent Yoshida and Tominomori,
two fluent speakers in the party, to the mansion of Lord
Sengoku, Inspector General, to notify him of the vengeance taken. Terribly surprised, he hastened to the castle
with the declaration of the retainers of Asano-Takuminokami which had been handed him, and after an immediate
inspection of Kira's mansion, an urgent council was held
by all the councillors. As most of them had been in secret
sympathy with the retainers, they were deeply moved by
reading the declaration. But though loyal according to
the code of the samurai, the Akô men were criminals in the
eye of the law, and it was settled that they should be placed
for the time being in the custody of four daimyô. So from
the Sengakuji Temple, they were summoned to the mansion of Lord Sengoku, where they were divided into four
groups and sent respectively to the mansions of Lord
Hosokawa, Lord Hisamatsu, Lord Môri, and Lord Mizu-
no.

There they were detained for more than a month and a
half for one reason and another, being meanwhile treated

very courteously, more like guests than prisoners. The
delay in passing judgment on them was caused by the
difficulty in which the Shogunate found itself because of
the almost universal sympathy shown to them. Even the
Shogun himself, who had acted so hastily towards Lord
Asano, hesitated to make up his mind at once. And after
taking the unprecedented step of putting the matter to the
vote of the daimyô and inviting the opinions of learned men,
it was finally decided to punish the Akô men as grievous
law-breakers by condemning them to death, but instead
of beheading them like common criminals, to allow them
the honour of committing *seppuku* as samurai. This was
a matter of course to the loyalists and they were all ready
to meet their death nobly. So the sentence was carried
out on the 4th of February, 1703, in the mansions of the
daimyô who had them in custody, and in compliance with
their wishes, their remains were taken to the Sengakuji
Temple and buried beside the tomb of the lord whom they
had served so well.

Henceforth the graveyard of the temple became a Mecca
of those admirers of the spirit of loyalty, and before the
graves of the forty-six ex-retainers of Akô, the smoke of
incense offered by sincere worshippers has been ascending,
day in and day out, for two hundred years and more.

CHAPTER IV

THE SPIRIT OF THE SAMURAI

Needless to say, the story of the forty-seven Akô *rônin* or ex-retainers is a typical one which illustrates the working of the samurai spirit nurtured in several hundred years of our feudal times. But as the whole trend of the affair culminated in the act of vengeance as inevitably as a body of water tumbles down a precipitous cliff, its versions have too often been given only with that point in view to the exclusion of the more delicate workings of the spirit as typified especially in the character of the chief leader of the band, Ôishi, an almost ideal samurai. And this has been sadly the case with the English versions which have already appeared almost without exception, from Mitford's first rendering of the story in his *Tales of Old Japan* downwards. For the right understanding of the spirit, however, other things in the event besides vengeance must also be taken into consideration, and it is by no means a needless task to point them out as well and find their significance along with that of the main issue.

Setting minor points aside for the present, there are three outstanding facts appearing in an authentic record of the event, and they are first that as soon as the Akô loyalists heard of the unfortunate death of their lord, they made up their minds to follow him to the grave as a matter of course, and eventually did so, secondly that in doing so they chose the way of avenging their lord's wrongs on the enemy in order to make their death of added value and followed it through to the end, and lastly that under the

circumstances they thought it their duty to strive first of
all to save their lord's house from extermination even at
the cost of giving up their revenge and did their best to
bring it about though in vain. Let us now consider these
leading points first at some length.

FOLLOWING ONE'S LORD IN DEATH

The Akô loyalists made up their minds to die on hearing
of the death of their lord, but, it must be observed, not
unconditionally. Their lord did not die of illness or by
an accident, but because of his indiscreet attempt at retaliation for the insult offered. His indiscretion was,
indeed, the direct cause of his death, which was inflicted
as a penalty by hands other than his enemy's. But these
were only attendant circumstances in the eyes of his retainers ; to them the fact stood unquestioned that their lord
died insulted. This then appealed to their hearts at once.
They saw that they must follow their motto with which they
as samurai had been impressed all through their days, that
when his master was insulted, the vassal died ; and they
gladly lived up to that motto.

But before expatiating a little on this point, it will be
well to glance at the unconditional form of following one's
lord in death, for it cannot be said that it had no bearing
on the matter in hand. This as a custom has a very long
history in Japan. In remote ages, it formed a conspicuous
feature of great funerals, so much so that in 16 A. D. an
edict prohibiting it was issued by the then Emperor Suinin,
and twelve years later when his Empress died, images of
baked clay were first used in the absence of human sacrifices.
But it seemed that the new custom slowly relapsed into the

old one till in 647 the practice was again strictly forbidden, and nothing more was heard of it after that for over seven centuries.

With the rise of the military class, however, the ruling idea that vassals must share their lord's fortunes on the battle-field, induced the revival of the ancient custom of following one's lord to the grave irrespective of the occasion that caused his death. This actually grew to be a military fashion in later years of the sixteenth century. At the death of a daimyô, it was then common for three or four of his retainers, nay, sometimes as many as twenty of them, to disembowel themselves for his sake. Iyeyasu, first Shogun in the Tokugawa period, was strongly against this custom of suicide, as is shown in what is called his " Legacy " or posthumous instructions,[1] and actually forbade the practice to be followed when his second son Hideyasu died in 1607. But his command was obeyed only during his life-time and after his death the custom was so much revived that in 1663 the Shogunate was compelled to issue an edict proclaiming that the family of any person performing the act should be punished. And at last in 1682 a clause to that effect was added in the penal code of the military class, which finally put an end to the custom. But seeing that

---

[1] The 76th article of Iyeyasu's " Legacy " which contains his command against the custom as quoted by Hearn is as follows :—

" Although it is undoubtedly the ancient custom for a vassal to follow his Lord in death, there is not the slightest reason in the practice. Confucius has ridiculed the making of Yô [*effigies buried with the dead*]. These practices are strictly forbidden, more especially to primary retainers, but to secondary retainers likewise, even of the lowest rank. He is the reverse of a faithful servant who disregards this prohibition. His posterity shall be impoverished by the confiscation of his property, as a warning for those who disobey the laws."

it was only forty years before the tragic death of Lord Asano, there is no telling but that the custom had a certain influence on the thought of the Akô men. Indeed, it had so strong a hold on the Japanese mind that even in so late a time as the era of Meiji, instances of such suicide, occurred once in a long while, and every Japanese remembers at least one conspicuous case—that of General Nogi and his wife who in 1892 committed self-immolation to follow the Emperor Meiji to the grave.

This custom of self-sacrifice on one's lord's death rose in all probability from the idea either that the spirit of the dead stayed where his body was interred or that it led in the world of shadows a life very much like the one he had lived on earth. So originally the things he had daily used in his life-time—tableware, weapons, trinkets, and such things—were entombed with him, and as he could not be allowed to go unattended, some of his family, personal attendants, slaves, and even his horse were made to be buried alive along with him. The monstrosity of the custom disarms our criticism, but it cannot be denied that there was an element of native simplicity in it, for though the practice ceased to be obligatory, it continued in a voluntary form, defying suppression for a long time. Undoubtedly the affectionate attachment to one's lord might drive one instinctively to such a desperate act at the agonizing moment of eternal separation. Ill-advised as the act itself might be, yet the idea at the back of it was, indeed, laudable. And who knows but that it was a mirror, so to speak, though blurred and cobwebbed from long disuse, held up covertly to a samurai to remind him of his inevitable course of loyalty in a most momentous hour of his career?

A samurai died when his lord was insulted, that is, he was bound to redeem his lord's honour even at the cost of his life. He died, of course, with or for his lord on the battle-field. He died when he failed to execute a difficult mission entrusted to him by his lord. He died even on making a clumsy mistake which might embarrass or displease his lord. There were, indeed, many cases in which a samurai was called upon to sacrifice his life in serving his lord. Extremely perilous was the way of loyalty with the samurai : he might as well cross a gaping abyss by a slippery log-bridge as follow the service of his lord.

But all this was a natural consequence of the samurai's being above all else a soldier under his lord. They rose as a special class for the purpose of standing by their chieftain through thick and thin. And as regards their duty in this function what Tennyson said about the Light-Brigade was equally true of them :

> " Theirs not to make reply,
> Theirs not to reason why,
> Theirs but to do and die."

So along with their training in fencing, archery, horsemanship, and other military arts, which was required of them in any case, was given that of the heart in order to make them hold their lives as nothing in discharging their duty. And, indeed, it was quite easy for them to be ready for death in the heat of battle ; but the contrary was often the case, even with them, when no urgent pressure except that of their conscience was upon them. So out of three hundred and more of the Akô retainers, only sixty-one at first joined the secret league, and though the number more than doubled afterwards for one reason and another, it eventually dwindled under fifty. This handful of men alone was truly prepared to die for their lord who was dead and gone. Such being the case, even Ôishi had the following couplet inscribed on the handle of his favourite dirk in order to be always reminded of his part :

" My lord's good will is weightier than mountains ;
    This life of mine is lighter than a hair."

The burden of loyalty, however, could be and was borne quite lightly by a samurai, for it was, as suggested by Ôishi's motto, based on his feeling of gratitude for his lord's favours. The relation of lord and vassal in our feudal times was far from being merely that of master and servant, but in virtue of hereditary successions on both sides, the ties between them were knit so closely that they grew to be something only next to, if not even more than, those of father and son. As a son owes everything to his father, so a vassal owed his lord the sustenance of his family, all of his property, and all the happy days from cradle to grave, and this not only for his own generation but for all the generations represented by the ancestral tablets to the memory of which he paid daily homage at his domestic altar. The loyalty then that grew out of such relations and was deeply rooted in affectionate sentiment, could go to all lengths in its service, and even death had no power to block its way. " The man," says Ruskin, " who does not know when to die, does not know how to live." A samurai was worthy of the name only so far as he knew when to die for his lord and if required, died accordingly with a smile.

A question might be asked : what did a samurai do when his loyalty clashed with his filial piety ? Instances of such a conflict are very few in Japanese history. But the famous case of Shigemori remonstrating with his father Kiyomori, head of the then powerful military clan of Taira, on his disloyal intention of displacing the Priest-Emperor Goshirakawa is often cited as such an instance, on account of Shigemori's confession that if he tried to be loyal, he would fail to be filial, and if he tried to be filial, he would fail in loyalty. But Shigemori's embarrassment rose from the fact that his father was disloyally inclined; otherwise there would have been no conflict. Except in such an extraordinary case, father and son were always of one mind as to their attitude towards their lord, so that loyality and filial duty went hand in hand; what the son did for his lord was most pleasing to his father too, and so even when an apparent conflict between the two duties might arise on account of the impossibility of performing them at one and the same time, the son was readily excused from his duty to his father, for that could abide its time or the father's claim on it would gladly be withdrawn.

Now though the spirit of the samurai as manifested in our feudal times was, indeed, admirable, as it was limited in its range by the very constitution of our society to the little world of their chief's domain, fears might be entertained whether or no it disappeared with the breaking-up of the old system, which came about eventually when the Tokugawa Shogunate was abolished. A samurai was required always to be ready to die for his own lord, but he was not taught to sacrifice himself even for the Shogun unless happening to belong to the latter's special military following. Much less was he given either chance or encouragement to take a wider view of such duty over and beyond the boundaries of his clan. In fact the policy of the Shogunate was actually to prevent his loyalty from developing into that larger one which is love of king and country, or patriotism as we understand now, for the obvious purpose of upholding its status against the Imperial Court at Kyoto, which was kept deprived of all its governing function. And as a risk of such a change coming over the mind of a samurai and his lord as well, (who was also a samurai in spirit,) might happen in passing through Kyoto, the daimyô were strictly forbidden to do so on their way to Yedo and back, and if they must pass there, they had to do so by way of Fushimi, swerving to the south and without stopping over. Did then the spirit of the samurai die with the age that is past and gone? In form, yes, but in essence, never.

The samurai spirit developed with the rise of the military class in Old Japan, evolving under the influence of Shintoism, Confucianism, and Buddhism a code which was military, ethical, and religious as well, but it was not entirely a new growth in its essence. More than a thousand years of Japanese history before the establishment of the military class in the tenth century go to show clearly the existence of a certain guiding principle which called forth the support of the subjects for the Ruler of the State. It took its rise in the way the national work was pushed on at the very beginning of our country when the Ruler started subjugating aboriginal tribes, perhaps with a mere handful of followers who were more of fellow-workers than dependants. The spirit of willing assistance coupled with absolute obedience and faithful attachment to the divinely descended Ruler, that blossomed out of the intimate relations existing then, came to be a sacred tradition with the Japanese through all ages and continued unextinguished with the unbroken continuance of the Imperial line up to the military age. This spirit called *Yamato-Damashii* or the spirit of Yamato, that is, Japan, which was more normal than the spirit of the samurai, as it had directly to do with the ruling Sovereigns, was, indeed, the prototype of the latter, which may be said to have remained temporarily in a metamorphosed state for the lack of proper development, but ready for better service later. That the *Yamato-Damashii* and the spirit of the samurai were one in essence may also be seen from many poems surviving from olden times; here we may give one most celebrated verse of Ôtomo-no-Yakamochi's (718–785), written long before the rise of the military power. He sang:

> " At sea be my body water-soaked,
>   On land be it with grass overgrown,
>   Let me die by the side of my Sovereign!
>   Never will I look back."[1]

This sounds very much like what a samurai would have said of his duty to his lord, though it is far grander in tone and conception.

The spirit of the samurai flourished under the Shogunate, but who could guess that it was this very spirit which was eventually to undermine the whole system of feudalism? The Tokugawa Shogunate collapsed as Japan faced the unexpected peril of Western aggression, but its downfall was caused not so much by its inability to cope with the extraordinary situation as by the awakening of samurai to

---

1   From the *Authorized Translations of the Manyô Poems*.

a higher cause, which induced the centre of government to shift from the Shogunate to the Imperial Court. And with the restoration of Imperial Rule and the abolition of territorial lordship, the samurai were no longer samurai but only Japanese subjects standing on equal footing and having one Sovereign over them all. By this change in social evolution, their spirit has been liberated from its old crust and returned to the time-honoured *Yamato-Damashii*, but much enriched and solidified for the service of the new age.

THE CODE OF VENGEANCE

The second point to be considered in connection with the Akô incident is that of taking revenge. Though vengeance lost its *raison d'être* at the promulgation of the Criminal Code and belongs entirely to the old order of things that passed away with the year 1868, as it constitutes the main thread of the story, the right understanding of its significance in the eyes of the people of the past ages is quite necessary to an intelligent appreciation of the story and the play *Chûshingura* based on it.

By vengeance, which was a social custom that went by the appellation of *kataki-uchi* in Japanese, is not meant, of course, any retaliation for wrongs done to oneself but only that part of it made by son or vassal for wrongs done to parent or lord. And though it was avenging of blood, as it was not mere individual revenge for personal injury, it does not repel our moral feeling on reading accounts of it even now. And added to this negative side, there was a positive one to it in that it was always an expression of unselfish devotion, of unchanging gratitude to father or lord so that it still appeals to us after all the many years that intervene between now and the past.

The sense of retaliation is so natural to man that it is no wonder that its higher application in an unselfish cause should have become recognized as a social obligation in early days. Of course, avenging incidents of this kind were at first quite few, but the idea was upheld and strengthened by Confucian ethics introduced to Japan in the seventh century, which more than affirmed this obligation, commanding a man " not to live under the same heaven " with the slayer of his father. The phrase quoted from the second book of *Le Ke* first appeared in Japanese literature very early in the eighth century in the famous history called *Nihon-Shoki*, and since then it became the unvarying motto for vengeance.

Even Confucius, however, did not allow vengeance to be enacted unconditionally : notice of the intention of taking revenge must be given beforehand and secondary vengeance was prohibited. All this was adhered to in Japan, as will be seen in Iyeyasu's injunction on the subject which runs as follows :—

" As regards avenging injury done to master or father, it is acknowledge even by Confucius that you and the injurer cannot live together under the same heaven. A person harbouring such vengeance shall give notice in writing to the district criminal court and carry out his design within the period stated in the notice. Secondary vengeance is strictly forbidden. Any avenging act done by those who have neglected to give preliminary notice of it shall be treated as a riot, and the offenders shall be punished according to the circumstances of the case."

Thus vengeance was sustained by law as well as by custom. But it will be observed that while in China vengeance could be exacted only for injuries to one's mother or brothers besides one's father, according to the *Le Ke*, in Japan one's lord or master came to be regarded as a proper person to be avenged, as well as one's kindred. This was, of course, due to the rise of the samurai class which grouped round this or that illustrious house. Thus along with filial piety, loyalty came into play in vengeance, making it assume a character nobler than when it concerned itself only with a family affair. Incidentally this fact goes to show more clearly than anything else the difference in the national character of these two people, the Japanese and the Chinese : there filial duty was all that was considered, but here loyalty had to go with it, or rather, as will be seen from what has already been explained, loyalty was regarded higher than filial duty even in the matter of vengeance.

Now, in the case of the Akô incident, the avengers did not try to give any preliminary notice of their intention to be entered in the official register, by which step they might be justified in the eye of the law and escape from being regarded as rioters. The reasons, however, were obvious. They feared first of all that by taking this step their intention would surely be communicated to their enemy, who in consequence might easily get out of their reach. They must avenge their lord's wrong on him by all means, and so took every precaution to ensure success. Then they had to follow their lord in death, vengeance or no, and why should they care anything about suffering even the severest punishment for a riot? Thus their act was, indeed, one of extreme recklessness, but at the same time was so thrilling and heroic as to be remembered ever after as a noble expression of loyalty.

Vengeance itself is brutal anyway, but there was much to be learned from the moral qualities attendant on it. It was impelled by unselfish devotion to lord or father, unchanging even after death, but in its execution it required the exercise of such virtues as depend on strong will-power. It was usually accompanied with all sorts of difficulty. The murderer felt at once after the act was committed that he would be the object of revenge, and so he seldom remained quietly at home but almost invariably fled to other territories to keep close at least till the affair blew over. It was no easy matter then to hunt him out and the avenger had to be a detective first of all, using all the patience and persistency he could muster. And even if this part of his work did not take long to do, he must look for a good chance to attain his object. This again did not usually come so quickly, for the murderer would be on strict guard and could not be approached by any ordinary means. The famous revenge of the Soga brothers, for instance, took seventeen years to accomplish. And though the circumstances in that case were quite exceptional, it was not unusual for two or three years to elapse before the vengeance was inflicted. The problem with the avenger then was how to tide over the intervening time. Usually he started on his wandering journey with some money, but as the interval of waiting lengthened out, it was as likely as not that he would fall into a sorry plight. What privations must he endure in such a case! In the Akô vendetta, which was carried out by a number of men much larger than in an ordinary case and took more than a year and a half in preparation, Ôishi foresaw this difficulty and wisely got ready a considerable sum of money to be

used for party expenses, but that even so it was not quite
sufficient for the purpose may be seen from the fact that
many finally dropped out of the league from the sheer
poverty to which they had been reduced. Under such
circumstances, it needed more than an ordinary amount of
persistency to carry their design through.

The persistency shown in the case of vengeance, however,
needs some explanation. It is not mere doggedness which
requires only strong will-power to support it, and varies
more or less with the persons concerned, but it is something
rooted in the spirit of the samurai and appearing constantly
under a different name in their conduct. There was a little
custom in olden days—a custom slight in appearance but
full of awful meaning—that in signing a pledge, a person
must invariably attach to his name a seal of his own blood.
The practice introduced from China was first followed only
by samurai, but afterwards became prevalent among all
classes. We had three instances of this in the Akô story.
The blood in this case stood for an oath, or to a Japanese
a solemn sign of promise, violable only at the cost of the
signer's life. As will most other practices, it was apt to
become merely formal and lose much of its binding character, but it was a visible form of the spirit behind it that held
veracity as the handmaid of loyalty. How veracity was
made much of by samurai will be seen from the fact that the
word of a samurai was always as good as his bond. To
give a written pledge besides his word for any promise
made, unless it was highly important and solemn, was
deemed quite beneath his dignity, and in few cases did this
code fail to work well. And if a samurai failed to keep his
promise, as happened on rare occasions, why, he atoned by

death for his default.   The persistency in vengeance then
was but another form of veracity so dear to the samurai, to
which under any circumstances he was in honour bound to
remain true.   In rising to take vengeance, he made a vow
to discharge his duty before the tomb of his lord or father,
and repeated this at the shrine of his tutelary god, praying
for his success in the onerous task before him.   And in all
probability, he carried a sacred amulet, given him at the
shrine, next to his skin.   So pledged and protected at the
same time, how could he break his vow and shamelessly
remain a samurai ?

   Lafcadio Hearn calls our attention to the religious
significance of the Japanese vendetta, saying that it was
essentially an act of propitiation as is proved by the rite
with which it terminated,—the placing of the enemy's
head upon the tomb of the person avenged, as an offering
of atonement.   And he describes the way in which Ôishi
performed the rite before the tomb of Lord Asano.   He is
perfectly right in looking on the vendetta in that light.
It was, indeed, done for the purpose of propitiating the
injured person in order that his soul might rest peacefully
ever after.   And not only at the close but also while he was
looking for the chance to carry out his purpose, the avenger
would visit the grave of his dead lord or father whenever
an opportunity to do so offered, and hold communion with
him as Ôishi did, truly conscious that they were speaking
through the impassable barrier that separated them.   But
such a practice was by no means limited to the case of
of vengeance.   With a Japanese in olden times, no day
began without his paying homage to his ancestral spirits
at his domestic altar, and every task of great responsibility

was usually commenced with prayers at the shrine of his tutelary god, which was, by the way, the deified clan-ancestor, and on conclusion reported with gratitude there. Thus his life was more thickly wrapped in religious atmosphere than are those of the moderns. No wonder then that the triumphal occasion of reporting the success of a vendetta should be celebrated with such impressive rites as the ghost of the person avenged was felt to be taking part in.

The Akô case, it will be remembered, was not one of ordinary vengeance. Lord Asano died, but not by the sword of Kira. His death was a punishment inflicted upon him for his grievous offence of defiling the Shogun's palace with blood. And yet he died without killing Kira as he had intended. For this then his retainers rose: their task was to take over his intention and carry it out in his place. This was clearly stated in their declaration given out for the justification of their deed. Now what does this signify?

The Akô retainers felt that they must be faithful to their lord even after his death. This was to them nothing but a matter of course. They treated him as if he were living; no, to them he was still living in spirit, waiting for his will to be done, and so they did their best to carry it through.

The belief at the root of their action was, indeed, the basis of the Japanese ancestor-worship. We never could think of our ancestors as dead and gone, dead to all the doings of their family left on earth, turning strangers to their children as the graves closed over them. Though invisible, somehow they love to stay in their old home, pleased with occasional, if not daily, offerings of their

favourite food and reverential bows to their earthly images..
And they stay not only to receive pleasure but to help, to
give support in promoting the welfare of their living family
by beaming encouragement on them.   All this might be
a delusion in a sense ; but the spiritual side of our life is
woven out of just such warm sentiments.   The beauty of
ancestor-worship testifies to its truth just as any great art
is endowed with life for that very reason.

THE CIVIL DUTY OF THE SAMURAI

At the conferences held in the Akô Castle when the
retainers heard of their lord's death, various resolutions
were in turn adopted.   At first it was decided that the
retainers should die in resistance of a siege.   Then they
resolved that they should merely commit *seppuku* on
delivering up their castle.   And the final resolution was,.
as we have seen, that they should avenge their lord's wrongs.
These changes, however, were not made by haphazard :
they were all premeditated by Ôishi.   His aim was to form
a secret league with resolute men, whom to pick out he
caused the resolutions to be shifted from one to another.
But along with this, he had another thing in his mind from
the first which was at variance with taking revenge, but
which he wished sincerely to be brought about.   And
this was the restoration of the ruined house and family of
his lord.   As soon as the first conference was over, he
sent messengers to Yedo to file a petition to that effect
with the Government.   Then at the delivery of the castle,
Ôishi himself presented another petition to the Government officers and spoke so appealingly to them that they
were greatly moved.   Again when he went up to Yedo

ten months after to prevent his party there from rushing into a reckless attempt at revenge, he did not forget to visit some influential men to ask their assistance in having his lord's house restored. We may well ask, which was uppermost in his mind, the restoration of Asano's house or taking vengeance?

Consider how he procrastinated in carrying out the design for which he had formed the league. Of course, he wanted to make the conditions most favourable to it, mainly by deluding his enemy into false security. And yet he did not hasten to his work even when his stratagem had taken effect. At the time of the Yamashina conference held at the urgent demand of all his men, who could hardly wait any longer, the opportunity was already ripe for action, but Ôishi checked their impetuosity by his earnest desire to see how his petition would be treated. He feared very much that any rash act would nullify his efforts. And it was only when he heard that Asano's brother Daigaku, the only person who might be appointed heir to his dead lord, was relegated and his hopes were utterly shattered with the news that he rose resolutely to the task of killing Kira. How patient he was to wait so long till the last moment amid the clamorous voices of his men urging him to vengeance! And all this was because of his more imperative duty of getting his lord's house restored.

Why then was it so important to save Asano's house and title from extinction? To understand the reason we must first go to our old cult of ancestor-worship and see what hold it has on the Japanese mind. We have seen that we Japanese never treat the departed as utterly gone, severed for ever from all their earthly connections, both material and spiritual.   On the contrary they still need our care and propitiation : we offer them things they liked best and pay them homage because we feel that they are pleased with what we do for them.   We consider that they can never find repose without this devotion of their kindred, the devotion to be repeated as often as possible by their living offspring and to be continued indefinitely by their future descendants.   The importance of attending to this service lies first of all in keeping our sense of gratitude and affection to the dead as the givers of life and all that we have inherited from them, but as they are thought to be always pleased with our being good and just, by remembering them, we take care not to cause them shame by our negligence of daily duties or ill-conduct of any kind.   Our filial piety is not due to our living parents alone ; it is also due to all our ancestors, who, though invisible, exist as spiritual presences.   So the neglect of devotional duty to one's ancestors is an unpardonable sin, while its discontinuance caused inevitably by the extinction of blood is to be greatly feared and carefully guarded against.

To a Japanese family, then, the continuance of its line is a matter of prime importance.   If so, it was all the more important with such a distinguished family as that of Lord Asano.   And then to Ôishi it was no other than the house of his lord for whom he lived and to whom all his service was due.   He could not bear to see it meet with a fate which was regarded as the supreme calamity to any family in the land.

Under ordinary circumstances, the extinction of a family line is averted by some means or other.   If there is no son to be an heir and only daughters, the succession is assured by adopting a husband to the eldest daughter. If totally childless, the family representative can adopt one of their male relatives or, in default of that, even a boy who is no relation just for the sake of carrying on the ancestral cult of the family. But ordered to be destroyed as the house of Asano was, there was no means left but reliance on a special act of grace which might be granted in answer to an earnest appeal.

While petitioning, Ôishi did his best to provide for the worst. Lord Asano had an only daughter ; and before she was relegated to exile, Ôishi secretly had her adopted into a certain wealthy family in Kyoto in order that her father's blood might at least be continued through her. Then he made donations to the family temples at Akô and elsewhere in order that masses for the dead might be held from year to year. But his greatest hope was to have the family line regularly kept on so that all the illustrious ancestors might have devotional rites performed by their descendants according to custom. And that was to be denied him. How crushing must have been the blow to the loyal heart of Ôishi !

We might ask how it would have been if Ôishi's petition had been accepted. The restoration of the house of Asano by such an act of grace could not possibly remain intact if subsequently the retainers took vengeance into their own hands, which would be rioting anyway. Besides it would be highly disrespectful to the Government to return its favour by such a lawless act. And Ôishi, who was a true samurai and was as sensitive to propriety as to the justness of things would not dare commit such an offence. At the Yamashina conference he said that restora-

tion and revenge were two separate things and that as the
Akô men might not attack Kira in force after their lord's
house had been restored, he would take vengeance alone
on behalf of them all. But that was said to appease his
excited confederates and he did not trouble himself as yet
to see what course he would take on such a mere hypo-
thetical assumption. Only he was sure to find the right
way in any case, and lead his men to follow it. And it
cannot be doubted that history would have given us a
totally different story if, indeed, the house of Asano had been
restored, a story none so thrilling as we have now and yet
bearing witness equally well to the sincerity of those loyal
men.

But all this is beside the question now. What we must
not fail to see in Ôishi is the firm hold he had on what forms
the ethical basis of the Japanese people. Success or no, it
is his faith in it that claims our admiration. He was of the
military class, and it was not to be expected that he should
take such deep thought on a subject far removed from his
profession of arms, in contrast to the conduct of most of
his men. They were all for nothing but revenge, that is,
fighting and having their sense of justice satisfied with the
sword, and had no time to scruple for a higher consideration. But Ôishi refused to rush on blindly and even had
the patience to wait till he was justified for his action. In
this he showed us what a true samurai should be : he was
first of all a man well trained in the fundamental belief of
his time and prizing it even above the demand of his
sword. To him loyalty consisted not merely in following
his master in death, but in doing what was best and most
imperative for him under the circumstances before he died.

And this leads us to a general observation on the duty of samurai.

The existence of the samurai or military class was a peculiar one. It was, of course, military to the bone : fighting was conducted only by samurai who were trained specially for the purpose. But they were not merely fighting men ; they had to perform civil duties, too, owing to a special organization of the government.

The sovereignty in Japan underwent a peculiar deflection quite early in history. With the rise of the Fujiwara family in the seventh century, the real administration of government came to be done only at the hands of its members. They grew to be veritable regents of the country and laid the foundation of the form of government which prevailed in the feudal times. The Fujiwaras, however, were not military and as they degenerated to a mere court nobility, the military clans Taira and Minamoto gained in power and after a bitter struggle between the two, the reign of the Minamoto regents first known as shogun began. They had their government seat at Kamakura and controlled the military and civil affairs of the country. And after the rise and fall of four more military families, certain members of which were shogun in turn, we come to the Tokugawas, much more stable than any preceding family but ruling the country on the same principles.

The peculiarity of the shogunate—and for that matter the same was the case with all the clans under it—was that all civil affairs were managed by samurai too, for they and they alone constituted the ruling class of society. But in undertaking such work, for which they had not been fitted by any preliminary training, they had to depend only on their individual talent in discharging their duties. Certain laws were indeed ordained, but they were far from being complete, and much was left for the exercise of common sense and discretion in managing business matters. Fears might be entertained as to the reliability of such methods of management, but being handled by samurai who prized honour and rectitude so highly, they were far sounder than mere obligatory functioning. See how Ôishi, in making arrangements for the delivery of the Akô Castle, regulated the loose administration of affairs conducted by his irresponsible compeer Ôno, by converting into specie the paper money circulating among the townspeople, at as high a rate as the clan's finances allowed. And again, see how he kept his account book carefully entered with all the party expenses he had defrayed out of the funds which were properly his clan's and not his own. Such fair dealing and honesty shown even when they were not openly required, were rarely to be met with outside the circle of true-born samurai.

The spirit shown by Ôishi concerning the restoration of his lord's house, however, was going a step beyond the ordinary fair discharge of civil duties by samurai. It has to do with the quality of statesmanship of which the true samurai was capable. The restoration of Asano's house was not only of invaluable benefit to the family itself, but also the prime requisite for the life of his clan which could be resuscitated only through that means. The grasp Ôishi had on this and the efforts he made for it deserve any amount of praise. A great statesman is he who never misses seeing the fundamentals of his nation's existence and upholds them at any cost even above the urgency of

immediate good. And Ôishi was just such a man. No
doubt he had inborn talent, but it was equally certain that
it was by virtue of being a true-hearted samurai that he
could bring it into full play.

THE CUSTOM OF *SEPPUKU*

The three main points in the story of the Akô retainers
having been elucidated, there remain one or two minor
ones to be touched on.   And one of these is the old custom
of *seppuku* or *harakiri*, which is self-immolation by disembowelment. *Seppuku*, like *kataki-uchi*, is a thing of the
past and, of course, does not exist now as a custom any
longer, but being only a matter of voluntary choice, it is
still resorted to once in a long while especially by military
men as something appropriate to them because of its
tradition.

This form of self-destruction made its first appearance in
Japanese history in the twelfth century with the rise of the
military class and became established as a custom with
samurai in committing suicide in the Kamakura period
(1192–1333). In the Tokugawa period, it was adopted as
a form of capital punishment for the samurai class and
upwards. It was, however, distinguished from mere
execution in that it was inflicted only as a punishment for
offences which did not go against the spirit of the samurai.
In such honour and respect was it held that in its execution
it was always accompanied with due ceremony, as seen in
the case of Asano.

It may appear queer that the abdomen was selected in
preference to other parts of the body as the place in which
the deadly wound was inflicted in destroying oneself. In

fact, when driven to commit suicide, Japanese women resorted to *jigai*, that is to say, piercing the throat with a dagger so as to sever the arteries, a practice decidedly more decent with them than that of the men.   But the fact that Cato, Brutus, Petronius, and other Roman worthies, as pointed out by Dr. Nitobe, terminated their earthly existence by this mode of death, will go to show that *seppuku* was not a strange practice even in the Western world but something proper to men of honour.   The reason, however, that it was accepted as such by the Japanese was based on the belief that the abdomen was the seat of the mind.   The idea is Chinese in origin, but Japanese mentality has been so much imbued with it that we have in our language scores of idiomatic expressions in which " *hara* " (abdomen) is so used figuratively.   To give a few examples, *hara ga tatsu* (to have one's abdomen stirred up) means to get offended ; *hara ga suwaru* (to have one's abdomen settled) means to gain composure or presence of mind, or to be prepared for something ; *hara wo kimeru* (to fix one's abdomen) means to make up one's mind ; *hi to no hara wo yomu* (to read another's abdomen) means to enter into another's mind ; *hara ga futoi* (to have a large abdomen) means to be large-minded or a man of nerve ; *hara wo miseru* (to make plain one's abdomen) means to show one's magnanimity ; *hara ga kuroi* (to have a black abdomen) means to be black-hearted ; and so forth.   So to rip the abdomen was a means not only of taking one's life but also of showing the clean state of one's mind, that is, sincerity, often in spite of the act for which one must pay with death.

The occasion that called for the sacrifice of a samurai's life has been given elsewhere, but even in dying he must not stain his pride.   And *seppuku* was just fitted for the purpose, for it required to be performed with the utmost coolness of temper and composure of demeanour.   Samurai were trained from childhood to behave so when required, and they were so true to their discipline that many who could do so, calmly set themselves to compose a farewell ode as Asano did, just before ending their lives.   Such refinement of self-destruction is nowhere to be met with but in Old Japan.

THE INFLUENCE OF THE SAMURAI SPIRIT

Japanese society in feudal times may be roughly divided into three classes, the *kugé*, the samurai, and the common people.   The *kugé* were Court nobles, standing next to the emperors and priding themselves on being their descendants.   Their duties, however, mostly concerned Court ceremonies and the grant and deprivation of Court ranks, and had nothing to do with administrative affairs, so that they were really men stationed " above the clouds," so much removed even from the samurai who ranked next to them.   But as they were true aristocrats, nearly all refinements in taste and manners in Japanese civilization took rise in their circle.   And so far they contributed to our culture.

Of the samurai class, which included shogun and daimyô, much need not be said here.   Combining at the same time the military and ruling classes, the samurai were held in awe by the common people, while they themselves, though somewhat unpolished in their manners, were dignified and set themselves up for upholders of the spirit peculiar to their class, than which for them nothing more priceless existed in the world. They regarded earthly possessions as trash and held dear the cult of the sword which was loyalty and honour. It was, indeed, fortunate for Japan that in the peculiar circumstances which vested them with powers both military and civil for hundreds of years, and allowed them to exist separated from the masses of the worldly lower class folk, they were able to evolve a high code of honour, severe and yet efficacious like their matchless steel, and be tempered and disciplined in it. They were the chosen people of society, on whose spiritual descendants the destinies of the nation shall depend.

The third class, that of common people, comprised farmers, artisans, and merchants. They were distinguished from the two-sworded order of samurai by not being permitted to wear swords or to have family names, farmers being called by their villages and artisans and merchants by their trades. Thus they were placed from the first in such a low stratum of society as to be far removed from the traditions sacred to samurai. They were looked down upon by the upper classes and their lives were held so cheap that any samurai was privileged to cut them down if they showed him disrespect. Of these people, farmers ranked highest, so much honour being given to them who tilled the soil and raised rice, the staple food of all Japanese. This came to be so also from the fact that in the early ages of Japanese society, there was no distinction between farmers and warriors : all able-bodied farmers were then trained fighting-men, ready for war at any moment. Indeed, a samurai might derive his income from land, as Ôishi contrived to do at Yamashina, and even indulge, if he had

a mind to, in amateur farming, while he was strictly forbidden to follow any trade or craft. Below farmers ranked
the artisans including smiths, painters, carpenters, weavers,
potters, and all the rest. Arts and crafts were held high
especially from the necessity of the samurai who liked to
boast swords of good make and also from the artistic
temperament of the Japanese to whom exquisite work-
manship with brush or chisel appealed as something divine.
Then came merchants, the lowest in rank according to the
order steroetyped in the categorical enumeration of vocations as *shi, nô, kô, shô* (the samurai, the farmer, the artisan,
the merchant). It may appear strange that they should be
placed so low, but the business of money-making was held
in contempt by the superior classes as something mean
and filthy. Indeed, it was not only far removed from the
profession of arms but was even liable to taint the soul of
a high-minded samurai by implanting in it the love of gold
which is the root of all evil. See how Ôno, who stood as
high as Ôishi as councillor of the Akô Clan, grew greedy
and made an ignominious retreat. Such was the disdain
of money among samurai that their children were brought
up with utter disregard of it, and ignorance of the value of
different coins was considered a sign of good breeding.
So though they created the wealth of the country, paid the
taxes, and supported the nobility and military with the
farmers, merchants had no chance of rising in the scale.
This, however, does not mean that they had no moral
code among them or nothing good in their life as civilians.
On the contrary, they had, of course, their own standard
of morals by which they transacted their business and,
generally speaking, they enjoyed a life far more com-

fortable and jovial than that of their frugal brothers of the sword.

Now what was remarkable about these classes is that on account of the hereditary succession of vocations prescribed and guarded by law and custom, class distinctions were so strictly kept that there was no chance of a man born in one class stepping into another, however strongly his propensities might induce him to do so, unless some such social reconstruction as the Restoration of 1868 made it possible. It was extremely necessary for national development that such barriers should be done away with and men should be respected not for the class they belong to but for the ability and merit they possessed, and especially that the spirit of the samurai reborn as that of Japan as a whole, should permeate the total being of all, both high and low. But the time was not yet ripe for that under the feudal regime, and Japan had to pass through some incubatory processes meanwhile.

But even in the Tokugawa period there were one or two things which showed that the spirit of the samurai, in one form or another, was slowly getting diffused among the common people, though sometimes quite abnormally. Just examine the following table which gives 103 cases of vendetta on record happening in that period.

Years	Cases of Vendetta	Avengers	
		Samurai	Common People
1609–1703	33	29	4
1703–1804	35	19	16
1804–1865	35	16	19

The year 1703 being the one following the Akô incident, we see that nearly all vendettas up till then were carried out by samurai, but in the next hundred years the number of common people as avengers came pretty near that of samurai, while in the last sixty years the samurai were fairly outstripped by the common people in this respect. It is to be remarked that the common people who so acted were nearly all farmers, only three of their number being tradesmen. Thus the practice of taking vengeance and the spirit that actuated it came to spread among the lower classes, making way for the reception of higher functions of the spirit of the samurai, and though few traders actually practised such vendetta, that their hearts readily responded to it will be seen from the appearance of more than a hundred versions of the *Chûshingura* that catered to popular taste from time to time.

How all this was brought about may be summarily explained by the fact that no social class can resist the diffusive power of moral influence. But we must look a little deeper into the causes which assisted that diffusion in this instance. The Tokugawa rule, which lasted for two hundred and fifty years, was conspicuous for doing everything to keep the social order rigidly undisturbed, fixing a place for everybody and putting restraint upon personal liberty from daimyô down to common people,—all for the consolidation of its own power. Ranks and incomes were fixed for life for the upper classes, occupations were hereditary throughout ; and even limits were put by regulations to the ways in which rich men might use their money. The common people especially were under pressure : however rich they might be, they must not imitate the habits, or assume the privileges, of their betters. They, more than those in the other classes, were bound by law and custom, chained to their position like dogs. But the long peace thus brought about throughout the country after centuries of warfare had its advantage. A universal feeling of security was established, and though bound and restrained in a hundred ways, the common people could without anxiety move to the length of their chains. And monotonous as their existence was, they could find solace along the line of least resistance.

In the first place the inexpensive and yet æsthetic accomplishments of tea-ceremonies and flower-arrangement, formerly fashionable only in the upper classes, came to be prevalent in their circle, while they themselves created plebeian music on the *samisen* and popular dancing to its accompaniment. Then, what was more important, literature also ceased to be the privileged enjoyment of the upper classes alone. Popular fiction in cheap editions came to be published to meet the public demand, and theatres and story-tellers' booths were thronged with young and old eager to be entertained. Now, what is noteworthy in this new tendency is the fact that the chief theme treated in books or on the stage was the heroic exploits of samurai in the war periods, of which Japanese history is full. These stirring or pathetic stories concerning the warring clans of the Taira and the Minamoto, the vendetta of the two brave Soga brothers, or the rise and fall of such great heroes as Hideyoshi and Nobunaga never tired the readers or listeners, and as these stories dealt with a world inaccessible to the masses, they were wrapped in romantic glamour wonderful and fascinating beyond anything in their prosaic lives. Thus they were led to grow familiar with the spirit that ruled in military circles, and though they were not in a position to follow it in every respect, some of them felt justified by it to take revenge after the fashion of the samurai.

The influence of the spirit of the samurai is also seen in the development of a certain order of men among the lower classes, known as *otokodate*. They, however, came into existence not so much by the diffusion of this spirit as through the resentment provoked by a certain section of *hatamoto* or retainers of the Shogun. The *hatamoto* were, of course, samurai, but they were from Mikawa, the native province of Tokugawa-Iyeyasu, and retained the simple manners and intrepid spirit of their country home. They acted arrogantly towards the lower classes in Yedo, priding themselves upon the fact that they were under the direct command of the Shogun. And some of them grew to be quite unruly and, banding themselves together, used to blackmail the merchants. Iyeyasu perceived this evil and in 1613 prohibited conspiring together of these men known as *hatamoto-yakko*, crucifying their ringleader Ôtori. But the arrogance and tyranny of the knavish-minded *hatamoto-yakko* were not to be repressed so easily and the lower classes continued to suffer accordingly for about eighty years more. Indignant at their contemptuous treatment of the lower classes, some among the latter, who came to be known as *machi-yakko* or *otokodate*, rose to oppose them and tried to check their rampancy. *Otokodate* were not, of course, regular and respectable tradesmen, but a rather lawless set, living mostly by gambling and spending much of their time in the pleasure-quarters. They made it their

business to take up other people's quarrels or to mediate
in them, and except that they offered quite a formidable
resistance to the *hatamoto-yakko*, they were themselves even
a nuisance to peaceful people and were finally suppressed
by the Government in the Genroku era.   But their ideals
were like those of the samurai after a fashion : they were
to help the weak and crush the strong ; they kept their
word with scrupulous care, and in the cause of justice, they
dared to risk their lives.   Unlike tradesmen or artisans,
they hated to work for profit and thought it undignified
to count money.   And though they ceased to exist under
the severe policy of the Shogunate, their spirit is still to be
detected in the true-born " Yedo " bosses of to-day.   The
type somewhat idealized will be seen in the character of
Amagawaya-Gihei, a chivalrous-spirited merchant, who
figures in the tenth act of the *Chûshingura*.

Plate II. A scene at the opening of Act I, in the curtained front of the Hachiman Shrine, where Lord Tadayoshi summons Lady Kaoyo, the wife of Enya. The characters are arranged as follows:—

Lord Ashikaga-Tadayoshi

Ishidô-Umanojô   Kôno-Moronao

Momonoi-Wakasanosuke   Enya-Hangwan

Lady Kaoyo

Plate II. A scene at the opening of Act I, in the curtained front of the Hachiman Shrine, where Lord Tadayoshi summons Lady Kaoyo, the wife of Enya. The characters are arranged as follows:—

Lord Ashikaga-Tadayoshi

Ishidō-Umanojō   Kōno-Moronao

Momonoi-Wakasanosuke   Enya-Hangwan

Lady Kaoyo

CHAPTER V

THE *CHÛSHINGURA*—I

Having given an account of the Akô incident on which the play *Chûshingura* was constructed, and some needful explanations of the spirit and customs of the samurai, we are now prepared to examine the play in detail and see how the Akô story is worked into it. But as the scene of that play was carried back some three hundred and fifty years to the time of the Ashikaga Shogunate, and incidents leading to the vendetta were taken from Chikamatsu's work, as already stated, and were not at all related to the historical facts, the play will appear as something totally different from the Akô incident and need a rather detailed narration of its story.

Act I. AT TSURUGAOKA HACHIMAN

The opening act gives what happens at Tsurugaoka, Kamakura. Having overthrown his enemy Nitta-Yoshisada, Lord Shogun Takauji caused a shrine to be erected to the War-God Hachiman at Tsurugaoka in commemoration of his success. It is the inauguration day of the newly completed building and the Shogun has sent his younger brother Ashikaga-Tadayoshi as his deputy to celebrate its opening. He is received by Kôno-Moronao (Kira),[1] Governor of Kamakura and the two officers charged with the duty of receiving guests, Momonoi-Wakasanosuke (Lord Date) and Enya-Hangwan, Lord of Hôki (Lord

---

[1] The names given in parentheses are the coresponding ones in the Akô incident.

Asano).   One of the items in the ceremonial proceedings
is to place the helmet worn by Nitta in the treasury of the
shrine.   It is, however, in a coffer with others, which
were gathered at the spot where Nitta had fallen, and it is
difficult to know which was his.   As Nitta's helmet was
given him by the Emperor Godaigo, the maids of honour
who were in charge of the armoury may be able to identify
it.   So Enya's wife, Lady Kaoyo, who was one of the
number, is sent for.   As she appears, the recitative chants
to the accompaniment of *samisen* music how, lightly pow-
dered and beautiful as a jewel, she comes barefoot on the
sand, the skirt of her overdress sweeping the ground like
the sacred broom of the shrine.

On hearing what is required of her, Kaoyo says that it
was, indeed, she who handed the helmet to Nitta.   It was
given him with a rare incense to be burned in it when it
was to be worn.   As Nitta gratefully accepted it, he said :
" Man lasts but one generation, but his name may endure
for ever.   When I go forth to battle, I shall burn the precious perfume in it so that if I should die on the battle-
field, the enemy to whom my head will fall as a prize may
know by the fragrance that he had taken the head of Yoshi-
sada."   And she does not think that he belied his word.
By the way it may be remarked that the burning of incense
in their hoods by the Akô men before starting on the raid
was prompted by the same beautiful idea of caring for one's
name even after death.

Be that as it may, Kaoyo at once picks out Nitta's helmet
by the scent she knows only too well, and it is entrusted
to Wakasanosuke and Enya to be placed in the treasury,
and Tadayoshi withdraws with them.

Kaoyo is now left alone with Moronao, who, seizing the opportunity, slips from his sleeve into hers a letter tied in a knot. Seeing it is a love-letter addressed to her, she is filled with shame and throws it back without a word.

Moronao now makes open love to her, saying that he is so powerful that her own husband's fate is in his hands, for good or evil. All depends on the will of Kaoyo. But she can answer only with her tears ; when at that moment Wakasanosuke opportunely returns and seeing that Moronao is, according to his wont, behaving outrageously, cleverly interposes and tells her to go home at once after her duty is over.

Moronao sees that Wakasanosuke has suspected something ; still he shows a brazen front and angrily says that if Kaoyo withdraws, it is by his own permission, not by Wakasanosuke's ; that she has been desiring Moronao, by her husband's secret wish, to instruct her husband in the proper discharge of the duties of his office ; that Enya, though a daimyô, has sought his aid, while such a petty fellow as Wakasanosuke dares to thrust himself in between !

The colour mounts into Wakasanosuke's face at the insolent speech and he grips the handle of his sword in wrath. But remembering that he is in front of the shrine and in His Highness's train, he restrains himself, when attendants enter announcing His Highness's return, and clear the way. The procession now comes in and passes on, with Lord Enya, little dreaming that he will be Moronao's enemy on the morrow, bringing up the rear.

The first act, of course, gives only the initial incident

out of which the tragedy in the third act is evolved, but in
all this the authors are following in the main the story in
the *Taiheiki* which Chikamatsu adopted.   It is briefly as
follows :—Princess Nishinodai was considered one of the
most beautiful women of her time.   She was given in
marriage to Enya-Hangwan, Lord of Hôki, but Kôno-
Moronao, Lord of Musashi, hearing of her beauty, became deeply enamoured of her.   He made love to her but
was rejected.   Piqued at her refusal, he slanderously
accused Enya to the Shogun of plotting against him.   The
Shogun believed Moronao and Enya was compelled to
fly to his province.   There he revolted in self-defence but
was attacked by the Shogun's forces and finally put an end
to his life.

The introduction of Wakasanosuke was, of course,
suggested by the existence of Asano's associate, Lord Date,
but it caused the authors to complicate the original story.
And the bringing together of opposing characters at the
outset before some important personage, though quite
common in other plays, was also the authors' contrivance
in this one.   The laying of the scene at Tsurugaoka was
suggested by another play just preceding it in production
though in that one the shrine was still building.

Now, apart from the consideration of the sources, if
we look at the staging itself, we are struck with the fine
effect of its opening act.   Of course, it may be staged in
several ways, but in what is considered the best one that
has ever been attempted we see the newly completed building of the shrine with its vermilion fences and gate aglow
in the sun, thick trunks of maidenhair-trees going straight
up in one or two places, and for a background the rippling

blue sea on which the islet of Enoshima floats dreamily, while yonder on the horizon Fujiyama rears its snowy peak in beautiful contrast with the blue of the sea and sky. In this various personages of rank in ceremonial costume sit or move, and the scene is at once enlivened by the entrance of a beautiful lady.   Notice that the lady enters not from one side as on the Western stage but from the *hanamichi* (' flowery way '), a long outer passage across the auditorium floor leading to the stage. This gives the audience time enough to see her well at short range.   The scene draws to a close with a long procession going along the *hanamichi* with Lord Tadayoshi, stately and dignified, as the central figure accompanied by many daimyô and other attendants.   The three chief characters now remain for a moment or two : with glaring eyes Wakasanosuke draws closer to Moronao, who tries to kick him away, when Enya scenting some mischief comes in between them ; and on this pantomime, epitomizing the situation, the curtains slowly close.

Altogether the scene is quite picturesque and the incident is decidedly more interesting than the actual historical one, for here it is made to centre in a love affair.

Act II.   THE ANGER OF WAKASANOSUKE

The scene is laid in Momonoi-Wakasanosuke's mansion.   We see a room or two of it facing a beautiful garden, with paper-screens all properly arranged.   It is now spring and some of the plants are in bloom, while beyond a large irregular-shaped pond spanned by a bridge of tasteful design, the view stretches in fine perspective towards the left.

It is evening and one or two servants are sweeping the garden, when Kakogawa-Honzô, chief councillor of Wakasanosuke, appears on the verandah. Hearing them talking about the insult offered to their master by Moronao at Tsurugaoka, Honzô admonishes them to be more discreet of tongue and sends them away as soon as their work is finished. Presently his wife Tonasé comes along with her daughter Konami ; they were attending on their mistress who, hearing a rumour that her lord Wakasanosuke and Moronao have had high words together after the close of the ceremony at Tsurugaoka, is now anxious about it. Tonasé asks her husband's help to put their mistress's mind at ease, to which he consents and he is about to quit the spot when a lackey comes up and announces, " Master Rikiya (Chikara), the son of Ôboshi-Yuranosuke (Ôishi-Kuranosuke)." Honzô guesses at once that he has brought word from his master Enya about the reception of guests at court on the morrow. So he tells his wife to hear what he has to say and inform their lord of his message, and as Rikiya and Konami are betrothed, to offer him hospitality. So saying he hurries off towards the inner apartments.

Tonasé guesses that her daughter would like to see and speak to Rikiya, and so asks her to take her place and receive him. But as the maiden still seems shy, her mother, under pretence of illness, so contrives that Konami shall see Rikiya instead. When they meet, Konami comes impulsively forward to him ; but Rikiya observes due etiquette, and drawing back formally delivers his message. He says that his master Enya-Hangwan informs Sir Wakasanosuke that they have been ordered by Lord Moronao to attend at the Palace of the Governor-General Tadayoshi next morning at four without fail to receive the guests. He has been sent with the message to provide against all chance of a mistake arising and begs her to report to that effect to Sir Wakasanosuke.

Konami is struck with admiration at the fluency of his speech and falls so completely under its charm that she cannot find a word to say in reply ; when suddenly the partition opens and Wakasanosuke himself appears, saying that he has heard the message and thanks Rikiya for his trouble.

Rikiya now goes away with Konami and Wakasanosuke remains alone, till Honzô comes in and advises his lord to go to bed as he must get up early next morning. Wakasanosuke, however, says that he must have some talk with him in private. He then relates how Enya and he have been charged with the duty of receiving guests in the inauguration week of the Hachiman Shrine with Moronao as adviser on ceremonial matters. Inflated with the high favour he enjoys, Moronao has become ten times more arrogant than ever and grown harder with Wakasanosuke, who is quite young in years. He has borne his insolence up till now but feels he can endure it no longer. He means to throw back Moronao's insults in his teeth before the whole court next day. His honour as a samurai is at stake. He desires Honzô not to attempt to restrain him. His wife and Honzô have often remonstrated with him for his quick temper but he can no longer brook these repeated insults.

Honzô is aghast at hearing this, but feigning that nothing is the matter with him, he praises his master's determination and jumping down to the garden, he cuts off a branch from a pine-tree, which he brings to the latter, exhorting him to cut Moronao down as surely as he has cut the branch.

Wakasanosuke feels relieved at getting Honzô's approval, and retires. Honzô now quickly prepares something and gives orders to saddle a horse for him at once. As the horse is brought to the verandah, he swings himself into the saddle and tells his servants to follow him to Moronao's mansion.

Hearing the noise, Tonasé and Konami come out and seeing Honzô in the saddle, so late at night, try to stop him by hanging on to the bridle. But the wise councillor scolds them away, saying that his lord's life and the existence of his house hang on his present effort. He tells them strictly not to say anything about his departure to their master, and he rides hastily off at a gallop.

The second act does not go straight to the quarrel of Enya with Moronao, which corresponds to that of Asano with Kira, but dallies with the anger of Wakasanosuke at Moronao's insolence, as if he, and not Enya, were going to kill Moronao. At first sight this looks as if suggested by the doings of Date's councillors, who bribed Kira profusely to win his favour for their lord, for here Honzô, councillor of Wakasanosuke, is going to do the same sort of thing for *his* master, as is shown at the beginning of the next act. But in reality this is the dramatization of another incident which happened before the quarrel of Asano, in which Kamei, Lord of Oki, who, bearing a grudge against Kira, was going to kill him, was prevented from doing so by a clever step taken by his wise councillor Tako-Mondo :

Kakogawa-Honzô being a sort of pun on that name. As this was done for the first time in the *Chûshingura* plays, it was so much to the credit of the playwrights. It may be noted that this episode was given to show a loyal stratagem often resorted to by faithful retainers to avert an impending calamity to their lord. To be loyal a samurai must be resourceful, as well as daring at the last moment.

The second act is given colour to by the meeting of the young lovers, Rikiya and Konami. This is one of the authors' inventions, nothing of the kind being found in the original story of the Akô retainers. The funny thing is that, while Chikara in reality was a strong, masculine boy, six feet tall, here he as Rikiya is represented as a handsome youth of seventeen, *l' amant de cœur* of his fiancée. To show them both here as betrothed is, of course, to prepare for the tragedy given in the ninth act, but see how the authors are endeavouring to keep up the interest by the introduction of a feminine element into their scenes, for this is done in nine scenes out of the eleven they have treated.

Act III. THE QUARREL OF ENYA WITH MORONAO

There are three scenes in this act. The first one is laid in front of the palace gate of Lord Ashikaga-Tadayoshi. A grand unpainted wooden gate raised on four thick pillars and ornamented with metal fittings stands open at the back of the stage, while old-fashioned brown mud walls with tile copings extend to the right and left of the gate.

Guests are to be entertained this day at the new palace of Lord Tadayoshi, built on his becoming Governor-General of the eight eastern provinces. The officials

charged with their reception are to come to the palace **at**
four in the morning.   First comes to the gate the palanquin
of Kôno-Moronao, lighted by four lanterns on which his
paulownia crest is painted and accompanied by his retainer
Sagisaka-Bannai and other attendants.   Moronao gets out
of his conveyance,—a haughty-looking nobleman, dressed
in a court suit of blue silk with large crests and wearing a
tall ceremonial cap.   Bannai bowing pays him a compli-
ment, extolling him above Enya and Momonoi, who, he
says, in matters of etiquette and ceremony appear as foolish
as a puppy dog thrown up on a roof.   " By the way," he
adds, " that wife of Enya has not yet answered you.   You
must not take it to heart.   Pretty as she is, she is beneath
your notice . . .   Well, you have expressed your passion
for her in verse, pretending that you wish to teach her
poetry, and yet she has not written you back.   But if she
really disliked you, she would have spoken to her husband.
As she has not, you need not despair . . .   Well, as you
say . . . . "

While the master and servant are nodding and talking
to each other, one of the samurai on guard comes up
hurriedly and tells them that Kakogawa-Honzô, the retainer
of Wakasanosuke, has ridden up and asks to see Lord
Moronao immediately, saying that he went to his house,
but was told that he had gone to the palace early.   He is
accompanied by a number of followers on horseback and
seems most anxious to have an interview with Lord Moronao.   Bannai cried indignantly that it is monstrous to ask
for an immediate interview with his master who is so busy
to-day.   He will see the man himself.

But Moronao detains Bannai and says that he under-

stands it all. Wakasanosuke, instead of coming himself to
wreak his vengeance on him for what took place at Tsurugaoka, sends this fellow Honzô to humiliate him. It is
some minutes yet short of four o'clock. He will see the
man himself and make short work of him.

So Bannai follows his master's wishes and tells the
attendants to get ready for a fight, when presently Honzô
appears advancing slowly as he arranges carefully the folds
of his dress. He is followed by several servants bearing
presents, which he lets them set down before Moronao,
while he crouches on the ground at a respectful distance
from him.

Honzô relates how his master Wakasanosuke has been
honoured by being appointed to so high an office by the
Shogun. But as his master is young and inexperienced in
the duties attaching to the post, he ventures to request
Moronao to advise him in the execution of them, so that
he may perform them satisfactorily. If this request be
granted, the whole house from his master and mistress
down to himself will be overjoyed and he dares to ask
Moronao's acceptance of the presents which are enumer-
ated in the list in his hand, as a slight token of their
gratitude.

With these words the speaker hands the list to Bannai
who reads as follows :—

" List of presents. Thirty rolls of silk and thirty pieces
of gold from the wife of Wakasanosuke ; twenty pieces of
gold from the chief councillor Kakogawa-Honzô ; twenty
pieces of gold from the samurai of the house."

As Bannai finishes reading the list, Moronao opens his
mouth wide with astonishment, unable to utter a word,

while he and his retainer exchange glances foolishly and stare blankly around them.

Moronao then has a private consultation with Bannai and deciding to accept the gifts, thanks Honzô for the trouble he has been put to. Honzô feels glad that his plan has succeeded, but still keeping his hands on the ground, says that as it is about four, he will take leave and entreats again that Moronao will assist Wakasanosuke with advice. Honzô now rises and prepares to depart, when Moronao holds him by the sleeve and asks if he would like to be present at the day's festivities.

This unexpected invitation surprises Honzô, but as he is low in rank and dares not venture into His Highness's presence, he declines it reluctantly. But on being assured that he need not fear anything in Moronao's company, he is only too glad to go in with him.

Soon after Enya comes up in a palanquin, and his retainer Hayano-Kampei (Kayano-Sampei) announces his lord's arrival. He is told by a warden of the gate that Sir Wakasanosuke has just gone in as well as Lord Moronao. Enya, getting out of his conveyance regrets that he should be so late, and hastens through the gate followed by Kampei.

From within the palace the sound of singing is faintly heard ; the words run :—

> " Harima's sandy beach they've touched,
>   Takasago's noted shore."

The notes seem to tremble in the drooping threads of a weeping-willow that grows hard by the gate. Near it now comes a lovely maid of about eighteen, O-Karu (ditto) by name, accompanied by servants carrying lanterns that bear Enya's family crest. But as they cannot enter within the gate, she sends them away and asks a warden for Kampei. Presently he comes out and, seeing his sweetheart alone, wonders what she is about. She tells him that she has come on an errand from her lady, and presenting a letter-case to him, she asks him to give it his lord to be handed to Moronao as her lady's answer. She is so glad that she was given an opportunity to come and see Kampei.

Kampei receives the letter-case and asks her to wait for him till he comes back after giving it to Enya. As he says so, a voice is heard calling out to him that he is wanted by his master. So he hurries in, when Bannai comes out with stealthy steps. Approaching O-Karu, he says that it was he that called Kampei away ; he wanted to see her himself. And he at once tries to embrace her. O-Karu frightened pushes him away. Bannai makes several attempts to hold her and at last, seizing her by the hand, he is on the point of dragging her away, when a loud cry of " Bannai, Bannai, Lord Moronao is calling for you " interrupts him.

Bannai reluctantly goes off and Kampei now appears. It was Kampei who has paid him back in his own coin by tricking him. He takes O-Karu's hand and looks about for a place to go to. Just then a verse of the song of Takasago is heard again—

"Beneath the pine-tree now they sit."

The words seem delightfully apt, and they go out hand in hand to a near-by pine-grove.

Here the scene changes by a little shifting to a large hall brilliant with golden partitions on the left and behind. The right side is shaded by large bamboo blinds. The

front and a part of the *hanamichi* are made into a passage
furnished with black lacquered balustrades.   Paper-framed
lantern stands are lighted and make the hall bright.

Momonoi-Wakasanosuke is pacing about the place on
the watch for Moronao, intending to cut down his enemy
the moment he appears.   Moronao and Bannai, unaware
that Wakasanosuke is waiting, approach the spot where he is
standing.   Moronao accosts him with civility, praising him
for being so early at his post.   Then he tells him that he
has a favour to beg of him.   So saying he throws down
both his swords at Wakasanosuke's feet and asks the latter's
pardon for having been extremely rude to him the other
day at Tsurugaoka.   He regrets it so much that unless
Wakasanosuke listens to him, he cannot, for his honour as
a samurai, take up his swords again.

Wakasanosuke is dumbfounded at this unexpected
change in Moronao's attitude, and though he thinks that
now is the time to kill Moronao, finds himself unable to
unsheathe his sword.   He only remains hanging down his
head in deep thought.   Honzô, who has been hiding himself behind a screen and listening to Moronao's words,
now grows anxious and peeps out to look at his master
for a moment.

Moronao now proposes to Wakasanosuke to go with
him to His Highness, but Wakasanosuke says that he does
not feel well and asks to be excused.   So he is given every
attention by them and finally taken by Bannai into an inner
room, to the extreme delight of Honzô.

Immediately after this Enya appears on the passage.
Moronao, seeing him, accuses him of being late.   Enya
apologizes, but hoping that he is still in time, takes out a

letter-case from his sleeve and hands it to Moronao, saying that it is from his wife Kaoyo.

Moronao opens the case and taking a piece of paper from it, reads out an ode written thereon, in which the intimation that, being already a wife, the lady cannot accept the suit of another man, is delicately expressed.

Stung by this rejection and growing angry, he bursts into invectives against her husband. At first Enya tries not to take Moronao's words seriously, but as more and more insulting words are heaped upon him, he cannot check his rising passions and, maddened, draws his sword and strikes Moronao, inflicting a wound on his forehead. As he tries to strike again, Honzô, who has been witnessing the whole scene, runs up and catches Enya from behind. Now all the palace is thrown into commotion. The officers of the guard rush in ; some surround Enya while others attend to Moronao.

Here the stage revolves, showing a scene about the back gate of the palace. A pine-bordered road runs from the front to the left, and paddy-fields are seen behind, stretching far to a wooded village beyond.

Great noises are heard in the palace, the front and rear gates of which are closed, and lanterns flash about in all directions. Hayano-Kampei, hearing the uproar, is uneasy on his master Enya's account. He runs up to the back gate and begs for it to be opened. He is told that those who are in the suite of noblemen must go round to the front gate. But he knows that the front gate is so crowded with retainers that it is impossible to get at it. He wants to know anyway how the quarrel has ended, and on asking

about it, he is told that for the offence of attacking Lord
Moronao, the first of the nobles, Enya-Hangwan has been
ordered to be confined to his mansion, where he has been
carried in a net-covered wicker-palanquin.

Kampei is greatly surprised and starts to run to the
mansion, but is arrested by the thought that the gates of
the mansion must have been closed, as required in the case
of a sentence of confinement. He does not know how to
act, and only paces up and down, when the maid O-Karu,
who was left behind, joins him crying, for she, too, has
heard all about the incident. But Kampei cannot be kind
to her now and pushes her away, saying that as he has
failed to be with his lord in time of need, his honour as a
samurai and a clansman is gone and nothing remains for
him but to die. And he puts his hand on the hilt of his
sword, but O-Karu stops him, saying that it is not for him
but for her to die, for it was she who made a faithless
samurai of him. If he, however, should die now, no one
will know his motives. So she invites him to go with her
to her parents' home in the country and wait there till
Master Ôboshi, chief councillor of the house, who is away
in his master's province, comes back. He can then ask
pardon through him.

Kampei sees the reasonableness of her advice and is
going to follow it, when Bannai suddenly appears with his
armed men and orders them to seize him. So they begin
to fight, but Kampei proves too strong for them and at
last has Bannai under his foot and is about to kill him. But
O-Karu stops him, saying that it would destroy his chance
of pardon. Bannai now wriggles out from under his
enemy's foot and makes off as hard as he can.

It is now long past four o'clock, the low clouds on the eastern horizon are whitening with the dawn, and the lovers hasten on their way towards the girl's home.

This is an act quite full of action and is sure to give delight to the audience by the dexterous management of various incidents. There are two cases of fighting : the first one between Enya and Moronao, though it forms the pivot on which the whole event of the play turns, is one-sided and not much of a sight, serving only to show the cowardice of Moronao, quite unworthy of his arrogant character ; but the second one between Kampei and Ban-nai with his men is quite exciting, forming, indeed, the subject of several *genre* pictures, Hokusai's being one, depicting this act. In Hokusai's picture even O-Karu is made to take part in the fight, though nothing in the text would bear this out. By the way it is well that actual killing is avoided in this scuffle, as such a thing would mar the tender sentiment that naturally goes with the flight of the young couple.

Comic elements are found in this act too. The tricking of each other by Bannai and Kampei, to the ultimate victory of the latter, is an emotional relief as well as funny. Honzô hidden behind a screen and watching the scene between his master and Moronao, excites the mirth of the audience by his furtive and unexpected appearance just in the same way as when, in a similar scene in *She Stoops to Conquer*, the parents of Marlow and Miss Hardcastle watch them un-observed from behind a screen. And the blank bewilder-ment of Wakasanosuke, highly strung to the point of draw-ing his sword and then unnerved by the sudden and unlooked-for obsequiousness of Moronao, appeals to our comic sense though the laughter is balanced by our sense of derision for the latter's meanness.

The character of Moronao is so skilfully brought out that nothing is left to be desired. His act of throwing down his swords readily at the feet of Wakasanosuke is such a disgraceful one for a samurai that it stigmatizes him as the lowest of his class. Even Kira would not have gone so far. Then his arrogance towards Enya as shown in the invectives heaped upon him, excited as it is by his chagrin at the rejection of his unlawful suit, is so great that compared with it Kira's insulting treatment of Asano seems but trifling. So much the better for the play that the incentive to bloodshed should be made so strong.

As regards that bloodshed, the part of Kajiwara, who arrested Asano, was very difficult to manage in the preceding *Chûshingura* plays, for the public greatly hated his officious meddling. Once an incidental character with no connection with the rest was introdused to perform this action; in another rendering a similar character was killed by the loyal retainers on the occasion of their final attack. It was to the credit of the authors, then, that they contrived to have this difficult part to be performed just casually, as it were, by Honzô, who happened to be near the spot and who had already distinguished himself by his efforts to save his master.

Kampei and O-Karu correspond to Sampei and O-Karu in history, but in reality they had no connection whatever. Nor had O-Karu been in the service of Asano. The true story of Sampei is as follows :—

Kayano-Sampei was the second son of Kayano-Shigetoshi, a retainer of Ôshima-Dewanokami. When twelve years of age, Sampei, at the recommendation of Ôshima, was taken into Asano's service as page. When Asano was condemned to commit *seppuku*, he was in the mansion of Yedo and set off for Akô to report the matter to Ôishi. After the dispersal of the retainers, he returned to his village to mourn for his mother who had recently died. As he lived not far from Yamashina, he often went to see Ôishi about their schemes of vengeance.

In the following winter he asked his father to let him go to Yedo and seek a new situation, but the request was refused, for his father knew that he was surely going to join the Akô men to effect their revenge. His father told him that such an act on his part would not only implicate his own family, but bring trouble on Lord Dewa, which the father could not allow, for he must be loyal to his lord as Sampei to his. Sampei asked his father to sever their relationship so as to free him, but was told that nothing worthy could be done by such an unfilial son. Sampei was at a loss what to do and seeing no way of avenging his lord's wrongs, he made up his mind to commit suicide and apologize to his lord in the other world. So he sent a letter to Ôishi to that effect, and killed himself. His father was afraid that if his son's death was talked about, the Akô men's plot would be brought to light, so he had him buried secretly. He was twenty-six years old when he died.

We see then that the love affairs of Kampei and O-Karu and their subsequent story are all fictitious, simply got up by the authors to enlist the sympathy of their audience. But in their eagerness to do so, they weakened the character of Kampei by attributing to him an act of disloyalty for

which there were no grounds in reality. Still, his failure
in duty for the love of O-Karu in this act was necessary
for showing his repentance in a later act, leading to the
pathetic episode in which she played a part.

Act IV. THE DEATH OF ENYA.

In this act the first scene is laid in an inner room in Enya's
mansion. The back and the right side are partitioned off
by sliding-screens which are ornamented all over with
Enya's family crest of crossed hawk feathers. Along the
left side a balustraded verandah stretches rather obliquely
a little way down the *hanamichi,* and a part of the garden,
beautiful with a large irregular pond and pines and bloom-
ing cherry-trees, is shown, extending from under the
verandah away to the interior.

Though Enya-Hangwan is strictly confined in his mansion in accordance with the sentence of seclusion, the
waiting maids of the household are passing the time
engaged in elegant diversions. Lady Kaoyo is sitting with
Rikiya, who has brought her a basketful of double wild
cherry-blossoms gathered on the hills of Kamakura. She
is arranging them in a vase, when Hara-Gôyemon (Hara-
Sôyemon), the chief of the retainers, comes along the
verandah with Ono-Kudayû (Ôno-Kurôbeye).

Bowing to the lady, Hara inquires after his lord's health,
on which the lady tells him that he looks cheerful, enjoying
the flowers in the garden all day. And so for his diversion,
she has had those rare cherry-blossoms sought out and is
now putting them in the vase.

Hara compliments her on her happy idea that as the
flowers open, so will the gates be opened and the order of

Plate III. Lady Kaoyo at the beginning of Act IV, arranging cherry-blossoms in the hope of cheering her confined husband. Hara-Gôyemon, one of chief retainers, followed by Ono-Kudayû, is coming up the covered passage to inquire after their lord's health.

confinement be revoked. He has come to tell her that the
Commissioners are to come this day with orders, as he
hopes, to set her lord at liberty.

But in reply to this comfortable forecast Ono tells Hara
that he views the prospect in a very different light. The
flowers are pretty to look at only for a short time, and then
are scattered by the wind. So with Hara's words. They
only give them vain hopes, for the gravity of their lord's
offence is such that it is sure to be punished with banishment at the lightest or *seppuku* at the worst.

Hara cannot bear to hear such words uttered. He
asks Ono if he is wishing for their lord's banishment or
death.

Ono answers that he, of course, does not wish for it,
but is only speaking the plain truth. Indeed, all this
trouble has been caused by Hara's stinginess. If he, too,
had thrown gold to Moronao, things would never have
come to such a pass.

Lady Kaoyo is much distressed to see the two quarrelling,
and says that the unfortunate cause of her husband's plight
is none other than herself. And she tells them how Moronao, angered by her rejection of his unlawful suit to her,
wreaked his vengeance on her husband by covering him
with insults and how Enya, who is hasty of temper, lost
command of himself and committed the offence for which
he is now confined.

On hearing this Hara and Rikiya show by their looks
how deeply they sympathize with their lord in his anger.
At this moment the Commissioners' arrival is announced.
Lady Kaoyo and those attending on her withdraw at once
to an adjoining room, the sliding-screens of which are

kept open, and the Commissioners appear even before
Hara and Ono have time to go forwards to meet them.
They are Ishidô-Umanojô and Yakushiji-Jirôzayemon.
As they are on official duty, they pass on without returning
the salutations offered them and seat themselves in the upper
part of the room.   Enya-Hangwan comes in with dignified
composure and bows to them.

Ishidô now demands Enya's attention to the official
communication he is about to give and taking out the
written order, reads it out.   It is to the effect that on account
of the crime Enya has perpetrated, his estates are confiscated
and he is ordered to commit *seppuku*.

As the Commissioner concludes, Lady Kaoyo and the
assembled retainers are filled with sudden terror and
exchange glances of amazement.   But Enya remains unmoved and expressing his acceptance of the command,
invites the officers to partake of some refreshments after
their labours.

Yakushiji now reproves Enya for his seeming want of
seriousness and also for his appearing before the Commissioners in his easy unceremonious dress.

Enya replies that he may seem wanting in courtesy but
he is fully prepared to follow the sentence given.   And
saying this, he throws off his upper garment and reveals
himself attired in a white, uncrested robe of death.   All
are astonished at the sight and even Yakushiji is unable to
utter a word.

Ishidô now asks if Enya has anything to say at the last
moment.   Thanking him for his kindness, Enya says that
ever since his attack on Moronao, he knew this would be
the result.   His only regret is, however, that he could not

carry out his intention of killing Moronao through the intervention of Kakogawa-Honzô. He is still possessed with an intense longing for vengeance on his enemy, and as Kusunoki-Masashige said at Minatogawa, he will return to life again and again to have his revenge on Moronao.

Meanwhile a confused noise of rapping on the sliding-screens is heard and a number of retainers beg Hara to be allowed to look once more on their lord's face while in life. So Hara asks Enya's pleasure. Enya thinks that their request is quite natural but says that they must wait till Yuranosuke returns.

He now makes Rikiya bring the dirk which has been got ready on a wooden stand and place it before him. He arranges himself in a suitable position for self-dispatch. He asks Rikiya again and again if Yuranosuke has returned. Hearing that he has not, he wishes Rikiya to tell his father how sorry his lord is not to be able to see him in life. As he can wait no longer, Enya takes up the dirk with the point towards him and driving it into his left side, drags it across to the right. Lady Kaoyo, unable to endure the agony of watching this heart-rending sight, turns away, murmuring in a broken voice the prayers for the dying.

Just at this moment a door to the passage is opened and Ôboshi-Yuranosuke bursts into the room where this scene is being enacted. After him hurry in Senzaki (Kanzaki), Yazama (Hazama), and a crowd of other retainers. As soon as Ôboshi sees his lord's plight, he starts and makes his obeisance. He informs Enya that he has just arrived and says that he is thankful to be able to see his lord's face once more while in life. Enya expresses his satisfaction too, and asking Yuranosuke if he knows all the cir-

cumstances of the case, says that he is truly mortified that
his enemy's insults are still unrequited.   Yuranosuke has
heard it all and can only beg his lord to die a samurai's
death.   Enya, taking out his dirk and now speaking with
difficulty, asks Yuranosuke to accept it as his dying gift to
exact vengeance with.   And stabbing his throat, he falls
forwards dead.

In the midst of the sobbing and grinding of teeth of
Lady Kaoyo and the retainers, Yuranosuke approaches the
corpse and taking the fatal weapon in his hand, lifts it
reverently to his forehead.   Then he wraps it in a piece of
cloth and puts it in his breast.   As he does so, he looks
resoluteness itself, the sentiments of unswerving devotion
and loyalty to his dead lord's memory swelling in his
breast.

The main part of the duties of the Commissioners having
been finished, Ishidô withdraws and only Yakushiji remains to see the house evacuated.

The funeral of Enya must now be attended to and his
body is carried in a palanquin to the family temple of
Kômyôji (Sengakuji).   Most of the retainers accompany
the palanquin, but Ôboshi and a few others, who are to
go there soon, remain behind in consultation.

When they have seated themselves, Ono-Kudayû speaks
out to the effect that as they are now all made *rônin* and have
no means of supporting their families, there is no reason
why they should not divide among themselves the money
their lord kept for military use and deliver the mansion
without further delay to Yakushiji who is waiting for
them.

Senzaki-Yagorô thinks differently from Kudayû.   It

arouses their anger to see their enemy Moronao still living, and so they prefer to wait till a force comes to dislodge them and make their last stand on their own ground.

Sadakurô, son of Kudayû, disagrees with Yagorô and supports his father's view.

Yuranosuke now intervenes and says that he is quite of Yagorô's opinion. They should really kill themselves and follow their lord, but he has decided to wait the force Ashikaga may send against them and die in resisting it.

To this Kudayû says that it would be reckless for miserable *rônin* like themselves to take up arms against Lord Ashikaga. In such a silly proceeding he will have no part.

His son chimes in and as it seems to him useless to prolong the discussion, he urges his father to go home with him. And Kudayû and his son take their departure.

Senzaki derides the pair for their covetousness and the cowardice they showed when they heard talk of making resistance. He proposes now that they should prepare themselves at once to meet the attack.

Yuranosuke stops him, saying that they have no cause to take up arms against Ashikaga. He said so only to find out the real sentiment of Ono and his son. They will now let Yakushiji take possession of the mansion and go each his way to meet again at Yamashina near the Capital, where he will unfold to them his designs and make arrangements for carrying them out.

No sooner has Yuranosuke spoken than Yakushiji makes his appearance and urges them to quit the place immediately. Hara apologizes for keeping him waiting and asks him to examine well what he is going to take over. And the retainers now reluctantly withdraw from the mansion

where they and their ancestors have served their lord and
his family for so long a time.

Here the stage revolves, showing the street in front of
the gate of Enya's mansion.   As Ôboshi and others come
out of the gate, they are joined by Rikiya, Yazama, Ôdera
(Onodera), and Hori (Horibe), who after escorting their
lord's body to the temple, have now hastened back to the
mansion.   The latter simultaneously ask if the mansion
has already been taken possession of.   They thought that
they were to make their last stand against Ashikaga's
force.

On this Yuranosuke tells them that they are not going
to die here and showing them the dirk his lord has be-
queathed him, says that they must cut off Moronao's head
with the weapon stained with their lord's blood.

The retainers are stirred by his words, when Yakushiji,
slamming to the great gates, addresses them scornfully on
their sorry plight, saying it is the proper reward for their
lord's crime.   Yakushiji's sneer is backed up by his
servants with loud laughter, which so much enrages some
of the younger retainers that they are about to break into
the mansion, but Yuranosuke stops them by reminding
them of the necessity of sacrificing everything to the
accomplishment of vengeance on Moronao.   Still they
cannot help glancing back angrily at the mansion as they
leave the place together.

The opening of the act with a scene in which mistress
and maids are tranquilly engaged in flower-arrangement
amid a wealth of beautiful cherry-blossoms is a happy

device to mitigate in a way the gruesomeness of the *seppuku* scene which is soon to follow ; or we may interpret the *montage* in a totally different light and take it as setting off the following scene by means of strong contrast between cheerfulness and darkness, happiness and woe. Either way it is quite artistically managed, leading to the quarrel on the symbolism of flowers, one view being quite humane but vain, and the other seeming cruel and yet sadly true.

This act combines two of the historical incidents : the *seppuku* of Asano in Yedo and the surrender of his castle at Akô. For this purpose Enya is made to perform the last fatal deed at his own house and not at another's as in history. And this is the more effective in that it is done in the presence of his lady and retainers, bringing in a note of pathos which was altogether wanting in the case of Asano, surrounded as he was by those who bore him no kinship or relation.

The contrast between the ceremonial costume of the Commissioners and the ordinary dress of Enya may escape the eye of Westerners, but it brings out strongly the opposition of the official authority which is to pass a one-sided judgement on Enya and the calm fearlessness on the part of the latter in facing such a verdict. The swift change of dress, a device often resorted to effectively on the Japanese stage for women characters, is quite dramatic here inasmuch as it takes the Commissioners by surprise, while it works none the less so on the audience too.

The death of Asano was quite lonesome, occurring in the midst of strange surroundings and only relieved by a farewell scene in which one retainer had a short interview with his master. Here Enya not only has many retainers near him but is met by his trusty chief councillor Ôboshi at the last minute. How enthusiastically the entrance of Ôboshi at the right moment, just as Enya drove in his dirk, was received by the audience at the first performance of the play can be well imagined, for none of the preceding *Chûshingura* plays succeeded in contriving so. It was, indeed, to the credit of the authors that they made this hit.

The meeting of Enya with Ôboshi makes it possible for him to give a command to Ôboshi to exact vengeance and bequeath the dirk for that purpose. This makes the motive of taking revenge much more direct and obvious in the play than in the case of the Akô incident. And it is much better for the play where clearness must be the first consideration, though we miss there on that account the moral quality of vendetta urged by the responsible sentiment born from the spirit of the samurai, the quality that is offered in history for us to appreciate. It is also noteworthy that the dirk with which Enya commits *seppuku* is made very much of in the play,—it is entrusted to the care of Ôboshi to take vengeance with, it is always made use of by him to excite his confederates, and it is finally used to cut off the head of Moronao. The idea is a happy one, but it is all the authors' invention and not grounded on fact at all. Asano's dirk with which he committed *seppuku* was presented to his assistant at that act, and the dirk with which Ôishi gave Kira his quietus was his own favourite one. But the story of Enya's dirk got so much hold of the Japanese that it was even woven into that fabricated so-called address of the Akô men offered at the tomb of their dead lord on accomplishing vengeance, the document taken as a true one by Westerners ever since Mitford translated it in his *Tales of Old Japan*.

The combination of Asano's *seppuku* and the surrender of the Akô Castle into one incident is a clever, summary dramatization, but it is a pity that the time allowed for the conference of the retainers is by it very much shortened. Consequently Ôishi's tactful manœuvring of the repeated conferences at Akô and the importance he put on the question of the restoration of his lord's house are both skipped over in the play, so that for the proper understanding of the Akô story this part must be supplied from history.

Act V. THE NIGHT ADVENTURE OF KAMPEI

The scene is a lonely one, showing a dreary place overgrown with thickets. A dark curtain signifying night shuts off the back half of the stage. By the roadside stands a low pine-tree under which Kampei, in a straw rain-coat and carrying a gun, is seeking shelter from the rain. A loud peal of thunder is heard as the curtains open.

Kampei has continued to live in poverty and seclusion in his temporary home near the village of Yamazaki, mourning over his disloyalty and gaining his livelihood by hunting wild boars and monkeys on the neighbouring hills. This day he has been out hunting as usual and now, late in the dark evening and caught in a summer thundershower, he stands under the pine-tree till it ceases.

Presently he sees a traveller coming in the rain with a small paper lantern partly hidden under his rain-coat. As he approaches the spot, Kampei cries out, asking him to give him a light. He is refused, for the other thinks he looks too like a highwayman who is waiting for wayfarers to play tricks on them.   But he explains that he is a hunter of the neighbourhood and is now in great difficulty because the tinder with which he lights the match-lock of his gun has been wetted by the rain.

Hearing the hunter speak in honest accents, the traveller scrutinizes him for a moment and suddenly asks him if he is Hayano-Kampei.   Kampei is surprised to be so asked and looks closely at the traveller, when he finds that he is facing Senzaki-Yagorô.

The two friends greet each other cordially after their long separation and as they naturally talk of the fall of their master's house, they are again filled with resentment against Moronao and clench their fists.   But as Kampei reflects on his unfortunate lot, he cannot but fall silent, bowing down his head on his breast.   At last he finds speech and says to his friend that he is so stricken with shame for his neglect of duty that he hardly dares to show his face even to so old a comrade as Yagorô.   He was overwhelmed to hear that his master had been condemned to death, all the more so because things came to such a pass mainly through his failure to be at his side when he was most needed.   He had once laid his hand on his sword to accompany his lord to the other world, but he was arrested from doing so by the thought that he had done nothing that entitled him to appear before his lord honourably.   He was wearing his heart out in thinking over what he should do in atonement, when it came to his ears that Yuranosuke, his son, Gôyemon, and others were plotting together to avenge the death of their master. What a chance that was to him, he thought; and ever since

then he has been looking for some means of getting a
favourable hearing from Yuranosuke and being permitted
to add his name to the list of confederates. How fortunate
then he is to meet Yagorô, and he cannot let go this rare
opportunity without asking his friend's aid in helping him
to regain the honourable position he has lost.

So saying Kampei prostrates himself before Senzaki
and, remorseful for his former ill-deed, bursts into tears.

Senzaki feels sorry for the man, but though knowing
him to be sincerely repentant, he cannot reveal the great
plot to him too readily. So he feigns that he knows
nothing about any such scheme as Kampei refers to. He
is now on his way from Yuranosuke to Gôyemon with a
message about erecting a monument over their lord's
grave. Being mere *rônin* now, they are all poor, but the
monument shall be such as will last for ever as Enya-
Hangwan's. And as he is going to collect the money
necessary for the purpose from only those who are still
truly grateful for their late lord's favours, Kampei, he
believes, is, of course, among the number.

The story about the monument is a fiction, and Senzaki
has merely used it to hint what sort of man Ôboshi is
wanting for carrying out his design.

Kampei guesses what Senzaki is driving at and thanking
him for his information, says that such a rumour has
already reached him and that he has been making every
effort to get some money to join in the subscription so that
he may obtain pardon on the strength of it. But his
present position is, indeed, a pitiful one. He thinks it a
fit punishment for his disloyalty to his lord, but he has no
one to whom he can apply for aid. But O-Karu's father,

Yoichibei, is a worthy old farmer in these parts. Lamenting that Kampei and his wife served Lord Enya unfaithfully, the old people are most anxious to see him again as a samurai by some means or other. If he tells them of his fortunate meeting with Senzaki and of the chance of regaining his former position, they will not hesitate, for the sake of their children, to sell some of their land. So he begs that when he has brought the money to Senzaki, he will kindly take it to Gôyemon.

Senzaki cannot resist Kampei's pleading tone and replies that he will tell Gôyemon all that Kampei has said and through him ask pardon of Yuranosuke. He hopes that he will hear from Kampei on the day he mentions. And he gives Kampei the address at which Gôyemon has put up.

Thanking Senzaki, Kampei on his part tells him where Yoichibei's house is and cautioning him against the danger of the road he is taking, puts him on his guard.

So they take leave of each other and go each his own way. The rain again comes down with sudden cracks of thunder breaking the stillness. Here the back curtain on the stage is taken down and a stretch of paddy fields with hills beyond is shown, while with a few shifts of the scenes, a gloomier part of the road shaded by pine-trees is presented to the view.

Through the rain and distant croaking of frogs, feeble footsteps are heard approaching. Yoichibei now comes tottering along by the light of his small paper lantern, carrying an umbrella and leaning on his staff. He is startled by some one behind calling to him to travel together on the dark road.

The speaker is no other than Sadakurô, son of Ono-Kudayû, who having been exiled from the parental roof for his wickedness, has turned highwayman and does his night work on this road. He now comes closer to the old man and asks him if he is deaf. He has been shouting after him for some time. It is dangerous for an old man like him to travel alone by night along this unsafe road. He is going to bear him company.

So saying, he gets in front of Yoichibei and stares at him rudely. The latter shrinks with fear but concealing it with an old man's tact, says that he would not have expected such a kindness of one so young. It is true that it is dangerous for an old man like himself to be out on such a night and all alone but there is no help for it. He is behind with his taxes and has to get some money. He went to his relatives to ask for help, but none of them were inclined to help him. And now he is going home without succeeding in getting a single penny out of them.

Sadakurô breaks in rudely, saying that he is not going to be fooled with the old man's nonsense about being behind with his taxes. He has caught sight of a pouch in the latter's bosom, a striped pouch, which, to judge by its bulk, must contain some forty or fifty *ryô*. Of course, the old man will howl about his poverty and the money being for his family. But Sadakurô cares nothing about it all, and since he has set his eyes on the money, there is no getting away for the old man. And he demands it to be handed over at once.

So saying, he snatches the pouch out of the old man's bosom. Alarmed, Yoichibei says that the pouch only contains some small cash left over after buying a pair of

straw-sandals at the last village and also the remnants of
rice he had for dinner and medicines his daughter has
given him for bilious attacks. So he asks the man to
hand it back.

And with a quick movement, Yoichibei snatches back
the pouch and makes off with it. Sadakurô, however,
soon overtakes him and as Yoichibei hugs the pouch in
his bosom never to part with it, the former draws his
sword and aims a blow at the old man. Dodging the
stroke, Yoichibei asks the villain if he really means to kill
him. On receiving an answer in the affirmative, Yoichibei
now tries to appeal to the man's compassion by telling the
truth. It is true, he says, that he has money on him but it
belongs not to himself but to his only daughter. She has
a dear husband, a *rônin* at present, who is in want of money.
And as it was through her fault that he became a *rônin*, she
begged her parents to help him to get back his lost position.
But as they are poor, they could do nothing. At last after
talking the matter over, they hit upon a plan to which they
got her consent. It is kept absolutely secret for the present
from their son-in-law, but she is to be sent to a house of
ill fame in Gion-machi to serve for a term. The money the
old man has got has, indeed, cost tears of blood to them all
three, father, mother, and daughter. So what will they
do, if it is taken from them? He implores the man to be
merciful. He, too, looks like one who has been a samurai
and will sympathize with them.

Thus Yoichibei pleads with Sadakurô earnestly, but all
without avail. Sadakurô, deaf to his prayers, thrusts his
sword mercilessly into the old man's breast and kills him.
The murderer immediately possesses himself of the pouch

and tries to count the money in the dark by feeling it. He finds it to be fifty *ryô* and is overjoyed. And hanging the pouch round his neck, he kicks the body into the valley below, little thinking of the retribution that is soon to overtake him.

He has not gone far on his way when a wounded boar comes rushing towards him. Startled, he stands back out of the animal's way. But just as the wild boar flies past him, the report of a gun is heard and he is struck by a double shot which passes from his back through his chest and rolls him over dead.

Thinking that he has hit the wild boar, Kampei comes towards the spot, gun in hand, and searches here and there for the game. Seeing something on the ground, he raises it up and finds to his great astonishment that it is a human corpse. It is so dark that it is impossible to tell who the man may be, but Kampei puts his hand into the breast to see if the victim's heart is still beating. In doing so, his hand touches the pouch which seems by its bulk to contain a great deal of money. Overjoyed at his luck, he raises it to his forehead to thank Heaven for what is doubtless its gift and makes off as fast as he can, distancing the wild boar itself.

This act and the next one form one continuous episode concerning Hayano-Kampei and his family. His secluded life in the country is, of course, based on the historical fact of Kayano-Sampei's leading such a life in his native village. But making a hunter of him and other matters in the episode are all the authors' inventions, though for one or two points they have taken suggestions from a preceding play of the

Chûshingura.

The change from scenes in high life to a rural one on a rainy night with thunder growling in the distance and gloomy bushes all around, is rather too contrasting, but the uncanniness of such a scene fits in well with the nature of the principal incident, which is too horribly tragic for broad daylight.   And the incident is very cleverly managed : old Yoichibei overtaken by a highwayman is a sorry sight enough, but his outpourings of blind and simple-hearted love for his daughter and her husband, endear him so much to the audience that his plight, when he is to be despoiled of all his money and his life as well, seems doubly pitiable. The deep hatred, however, aroused in the audience for the wicked man is soon appeased by the swift retribution that descends on him, and that through the hands of the old man's son-in-law himself.

Some may think that Kampei's stealing the pouch alienates any sympathy they have felt with his lot, but this is not necessarily the case.   It reiterates the fact that he is a man not very strong in character anyway, and though good at heart he is liable to come to grief.   The tragedy of his life is due primarily to that weakness in him.

The selling of a girl to a brothel is disgusting to modern minds, but it was an evil practice often formerly resorted to among the lower classes when much in need of money, and as such we might pass it over in our enjoyment of classic literature.   But indeed, as it says in the play that the money got by the transaction has cost tears of blood to those concerned, so we see the act was regarded as something extremely heart-rending and tragic, though we might not feel so on first hearing of it.

Act VI. THE DEATH OF KAMPEI

On the stage stands the weather-beaten thatched cottage
of a peasant with a well on its left and beside it a tub and
a wooden pail are left ready for use.   The paper sliding-
screens in front and on one side have been removed for
coolness, except for the old-looking ones that partition
off an inner room, near which O-Karu sits before a simple
toilet-stand to dress her hair.   She is beautiful to look at,
too fair, indeed, for such a rural spot.   As she finishes her
task, her old mother, O-Kaya, leaning on a stick, comes
tottering home from the fields.

O-Kaya admires her daughter's toilet and tells her that
everywhere in the village, the corn-harvest is being gathered
in and people are as busy as they can be.   Not far away by
the bamboo copse they hear young fellows singing—

" The harvest-dance is going on,
　　Come out, old man, come with your dame."

At the words her heart throbs with sudden anxiety, for *her*
' old man' is late returning home.   She now goes as far as
the end of the village to look out for him, but not a
shadow of him can be seen.

O-Karu says that she is wondering, too, what can make
him so late.   She will just run out and see if he is coming.

But her mother stops her, saying that it is not well for
a young woman to go wandering about all alone.   She
remembers that O-Karu never liked from her childhood
to walk about the village.   That was partly why they sent
her to service at Lord Enya's.   And though she is back
again in the lonely country, she looks happy only because
she is with Kampei.

O-Karu agrees with her mother and says that when a girl has her lover with her, however dull the village, or however poor they may be, all seems joyous to her. And when the Feast of Lanterns comes, she means to do as the old song says, " Come out, old man, come with your dame," and go with Kampei to see the dance. She is sure that her mother, too, did that sort of thing in her youth.

The girl chatters on lightly, wishing to spare her mother any anxiety, but she cannot hide completely the restlessness of her heart. The mother is not slow to guess her daughter's true feelings, but the latter assures her that she is not troubled. She is quite ready to go to service in Gion-machi, for that is for the sake of her dear husband ; but what grieves her is the thought that she will no longer be able to look after her father's comforts. The mother tells her daughter to be at ease on that point, for low as his position is, her brother is a servant of Lord Enya too and will do what he can for his aged father.

As mother and daughter are talking thus, there arrives Ichimonjiya, the master of a tea-house in Gion-machi, with a palanquin carried by two coolies. He comes up to the door and asks if Yoichibei is at home.

As he has been here before, O-Kaya recognizes him at once and asks him in. After greeting the woman Ichi-monjiya thanks her for the trouble her husband took in calling on him the previous night and hopes that he has got back all right. The woman replies, with a look of surprise, that he has not. The tea-house master is surprised, too, at hearing this, but as there is no help for it now, he tells her that he has come to take away the girl according to the agreement. Yoichibei and he decided last night that she should serve in the house for five years for a payment of one hundred *ryô*. As Yoichibei then said that he was in pressing need of the money and begged to have it now in advance, Ichimonjiya gave him half the sum when the paper was signed and sealed, promising to pay the remainder on the delivery of the girl. Yoichibei was overjoyed when he was handed the fifty *ryô* and although it was so late as ten o'clock he set out on his return journey. Ichimonjiya warned the old man that it was not safe to travel by night with money about him, but he would not listen to him and hurried off. Perhaps he had stopped somewhere on the road.

But as there is no place he would be likely to stop at, the old woman and her daughter cannot understand his being so long.

The tea-house master says that, whether they understand it or not, that is their affair. He will hand over the balance and take the girl with him.

O-Kaya, however, says that she cannot give her daughter up until the old man shall have returned.

Ichimonjiya is now impatient : he cannot waste time. The bond with Yoichibei's seal on it speaks for itself. The girl is his from this day ; a day's delay means so much loss to him. She must and shall go with him. So saying, he seizes O-Karu by the hand and gets her to the palanquin in spite of her mother's resistance.

At this crisis Kampei, gun on shoulder and with a straw rain-coat on, suddenly makes his appearance. Seeing his wife in a palanquin, he wonders where she is going. The girl's mother cries that she is so glad that Kampei has come ; he is just in time. Kampei cannot understand her delight and thinking that there must be some mystery here, demands an explanation.

At this Ichimonjiya, guessing Kampei to be the girl's husband and wishing to prevent any further fuss, brings out the bond and, pointing to Yoichibei's seal, says that husband or not matters little to him, for it is provided in the contract that no one whatever shall prevent it from being carried out.   And he is going to take away the girl at once.

Here O-Kaya says that she must explain to Kampei. Their daughter told them that Kampei was in great need of money and begged them to give her some for him, but much as they wished to do so, they had no prospect of getting any.   At last her father said that the only way was to send their daughter for a time to service in the licensed quarters.   He thought that Kampei would not be angry with him if by that means he came into possession of the money he needed for his lord's cause.   But as it was better to do so without Kampei's knowledge, his father went yesterday to a tea-house in Gion-machi to settle the matter. The old man has not returned yet, which makes them feel very anxious about him.   In the midst of their anxiety, the gentleman now before him comes and says that as he gave the old man fifty *ryô* last night, he has brought the remaining fifty *ryô* which he offers to them in exchange for O-Karu. She has asked him to wait for the old man's return but he will not listen to her.   She asks Kampei what they are to do.

Kampei expresses his gratitude for his father-in-law's kindness and adds that he, too, has had a piece of good fortune, but of that he will speak by and by.   He is of a

mind that they had better wait for the old man before handing over his wife.   Perhaps what the man says is true but
it is better to be very cautious in such matters.

At this Ichimonjiya cannot remain silent and he tells
them that he has a fine large business with plenty of credit
—he is not the man to say that he has done what he has not !
And for a further proof that he has paid half the money, he
says that when he gave it to the old man, he lent him a
pouch made of the same piece of striped cloth as the dress
he now has on.   No doubt the old man will presently come
home with it round his neck.

Kampei is amazed to hear the last part of the man's talk.
He stealthily takes out the pouch he has with him, and
seeing that it is of exactly the same stuff as that of the
speaker's dress, he cannot but conclude that the man he
accidently killed was his own father-in-law.

He remains speechless for a while, when urged by his
wife coming out of the palanquin to tell her what she is to
do, he says that as there appears to be no help for it, she
must go with the man.   O-Karu regrets that she has to go
without seeing her father.   On this, to put her mind at
ease, Kampei says that he forgot to tell them before but he
saw the old man this morning, though it is uncertain when
he will return.   It is news to them and O-Karu reproaches
Kampei for not saying so at once and putting an end to
their anxiety.

Ichimonjiya, who has been waiting impatiently so far,
takes advantage of this moment and says that now that the
whereabouts of the old man is known, there is nothing that
prevents him further from taking O-Karu with him.   And
so the poor girl is made to get into the palanquin again and

is carried away while her mother is crying bitterly and she herself miserably sobbing.

O-Kaya, left alone with Kampei, her simple heart full of grief for her daughter, sympathy for her son-in-law, and anxiety for her husband, now begins to question Kampei about the place where he said that he met the old man, but without getting any definite answer, when three hunters of the neighbourhood come up, bearing on a shutter Yoichibei's body. They say that they found his murdered corpse as they came home from hunting last night.

O-Kaya is overwhelmed at the unexpected sight and for the moment is bereft of speech. Then she weeps as if her heart would break over the old man's remains. The hunters are shocked at the sight of her misery and soon take their departure, after attempting a few words of condolence.

The old woman, somewhat composed, is now filled with resentment and urges Kampei to find out the murderer and take revenge on him. But as it strikes her that Kampei shows strangely little amazement at the sight of his father-in-law's corpse, a monstrous suspicion creeps into her mind, and suddenly putting her hand into Kampei's breast she draws out the pouch. She says that she saw him looking at it furtively a while ago, and since it is stained with blood, to her horror, she feels that Kampei must be the person who killed her old man. She now heaps all sorts of curses upon him, reviling him for a villainous, inhuman monster, while Kampei sits dumbly with no words to contradict her. In her fury she seizes him by the hair and buffets him with all her might, and Kampei, in an agony

of remorse, clings to the mat, feeling that the judgment of
Heaven has come upon him.

Just at this moment two samurai wearing deep wicker-
hats arrive at the door.   They are Hara-Gôyemon and
Senzaki-Yagorô who have come to see Kampei.   Ill-
timed as their visit is, Kampei rises to receive them and
thanks them for so honouring his humble home.   He
kneels before them and apologizing to them for his failure
in duty, entreats them to intercede for him so that he may
be permitted to join with the other retainers in com-
memorating the anniversary of their late lord's death.

Hara says in reply that they have received Kampei's
subscription of a large amount towards the expense of
raising a monument to their dead lord.   Yuranosuke has
been informed of this, but Kampei's disloyalty makes it
impossible for him to accept it.   So they have been ordered
to return it to him.   With these words Hara tells Senzaki
to take out a paper packet containing the money Kampei
handed him early in the morning and place it before the
youth, who, wild with grief and despair at the ruin of his
hopes, is unable to utter a word.

O-Kaya, who has been watching the interview, at this
point comes forward and says that Kampei is now reaping
his reward.   She tells the guests how Kampei's father-in-
law sold his daughter into service for the sake of the young
man and how the latter, lying in wait for the old man as he
came home in the dark with the money, murdered him and
robbed him of it.   The money is tainted and they have
done well to return it.   Kampei is a robber and parricide
and she desires them to strike him with their swords and
kill him inch by inch.

With this the old woman throws herself on the floor in a flood of tears.   Hara and Senzaki reproach Kampei one after the other in such bitter words that the young man driven to the extremity of despair sees but one course open to him and, suddenly baring his shoulders, draws his dirk and plunges it into his bowels.   As he does so, he says that he was prepared to kill himself if his desire could not be attained.   At the last moment he wishes to explain how he came to murder his father-in-law, and tells how by shooting a wild boar he accidentally killed a wayfarer and then found a pouch in his breast, which, though possibly he did wrong in taking it, seemed to him at the moment to be sent to him from Heaven.   So hurrying after Senzaki with it, he gave the contents and came home, when he found that the man he had killed was his father-in-law and the money was the price of his wife.   Thus everything he did has gone amiss and his doom is sealed.   He begs his visitors to spare him at least a little sympathy.

Senzaki, as if struck by a sudden thought, rises up hastily to examine the corpse and turning it over, finds a gash on it.   It looks at first like a gunshot wound, but really it is a sword cut.   Kampei has been, indeed, overhasty.

O-Kaya is so astonished by the discovery that she cannot utter a word.

Hara remembers now that he with Senzaki passed a corpse in coming here with a gunshot wound on it.   They found that it was the body of Ono-Sadakurô, a villain whom even his father, though a covetous wretch himself, had to disown.   It was said that he had turned highwayman. Without doubt the murderer of Kampei's father-in-law was no other than he.

O-Kaya, now convinced of her mistake, clings to Kampei and asking his forgiveness, begs him not to die ; while Kampei, glad that he is cleared of suspicions, says that he can now depart in peace and meet his father-in-law in the other world.   He is going to hasten his death, when Hara arrests his hand and tells him that, though without knowing it, he has taken a glorious revenge for his father-in-law's death ; thus fortune has not been all against him.   And saying that he has something to show to Kampei before he dies, Hara takes out from his breast a scroll on which the convenant is written, signed by the confederates who have sworn to slay their lord's enemy, Moronao.   There are forty-five names on it, but now that Kampei's spirit is clearly known, his name will be added to the list.

Great is Kampei's joy on hearing this, and he thanks Hara and Senzaki for enabling him to obtain what he has most wished for in the world.   He hopes that the money will be used advantageously for the purpose of carrying out their plot.

O-Kaya presents the pouch, which Hara accepts, saying that they will prize it as if it were full of gold.   It will accompany them when they are going to attack the enemy.

Kampei says that though he dies, his spirit shall remain on earth and be with the confederates till their object is attained ; and so saying he pierces his throat with his dirk and, falling forward, dies.

O-Kaya now bursts into loud lamentations ; so pitiable is the sight that Hara and Senzaki do not know how to comfort her.   At last Hara says that her lot must be, indeed, hard to bear, but it may comfort her if he tells her that he is going to inform Ôboshi of the manner of Kampei's

death.   And he thinks that she had better keep the money,
a hundred *ryô* in all, for offering prayers and holding services
for the repose of the souls of her husband and son-in-law.

And they take their leave, accepting only the pouch as a
sign of another faithful confederate having joined their
league.   Tears in the eyes of the old woman, tears in the
eyes of the two samurai, they part, perhaps never to meet
again, but with their hearts glowing warm in the true
kindliness of life.

This act forms with the preceding one a play within
the play and is very cleverly executed though the scene is
simple and rustic with nothing impressive about it as in
the other acts.   The complications in the plot and their
skilful unravelling leading to an end which is quite satisfactory under the circumstances are something that makes
the audience follow it with breathless interest from beginning to end.   Along with the repeated use of surprise,
occasions for deep grief abound ; indeed, except for the
opening of the act, which is in somewhat lighter vein,
—though this is, in fact, only camouflaging the rising
anxiety and heaviness of heart on the part of the two loving
souls—the act is one continuous outburst of sorrow, so
pathetic that the audience cannot but be moved to tears
throughout.

It may be said to the credit of the authors, too, that
though in the early part O-Karu figures as a pathetic character, making her mother's heart overflow with tender
affection, she is spared the excruciating sadness of facing
the death of her father and husband, which would be too
cruel for her.   From the shameful nature of the service

she is going to engage in, one may be inclined to depreciate her character, but she thinks of herself only as a sacrifice willingly offered for the sake of her dear husband, which is an act no less heroic than that of laying down one's life for one's master.   At any rate she stands as yet like a rose in its first bloom, a girl not only lovely in appearance but sweet and affectionate at heart.

The Sampei of history was driven into a dilemma in which filial piety and loyalty clashed with each other.   But he committed self-dispatch not so much to escape from the agony of finding himself in such a stress as to show his determination to follow the path of loyalty at any cost, for to live on as he was would evidently have meant his prefer-ence of being filial to his father to being faithful to his lord. Kampei's *seppuku* looks at the first blush like an atone-ment for his theft and parricide, and no doubt there is much of this, too, in his act ; but as the miscarriage of the means is tantamount to the hopelessness of gaining his end, he is more chagrined with the second than the first.   And seeing that, in fact, he had made ready, as he avows, for the inevitable in case his subscription was rejected, before what was supposed to be his crime was known to Hara and Senzaki, his self-immolation is much in the same vein as that of Sampei,—an expression of his indomitable will to serve his lord in spite of the barriers which could not be broken through but with his death.   The spirit of the samurai is as well exhibited in his case as in that of his historical prototype.

The *dénouement* of the episode is very well contrived. The addition of Kampei's name to the list of confederates, though not grounded in history, signifies, of course, the

recognition of his loyal and devoted spirit and is as much
to his honour as to the satisfaction of the audience. He
dies, but is made to achieve in spirit what he most wished
in life. And the return of the money offered by Kampei to
be used for holding services for the repose of the two souls
accords well with the spirit of the samurai, who was brave
and loyal on the one hand and pious on the other.

CHAPTER VI

THE *CHÛSHINGURA*—II

Act VII. YURANOSUKE LEADS A DISSOLUTE LIFE

The scene is laid in Ichimonjiya's fashionable tea-house Ichiriki in Gion-machi, Kyoto. A room with a verandah facing the garden and a part of the balustraded upper verandah looking down to it are shown. There is an artistic iron-framed lantern hanging at one end, under which a large water-basin is placed on a natural stone stand; stepping-stones lead from the lower verandah to a wicket at one side of the garden. Everything is tastefully arranged as befits this stylish building. A few red-aproned waitresses are singing a ballad merrily in the garden as the curtains open.

Here two guests come in through the wicket. They are Ono-Kudayû and Sagisaka-Bannai; they want a room where they can have a quiet drop together. They are told that this evening a rich gentleman named Yuranosuke has brought together all the well-known women of the place and is occupying the whole of the ground floor, but they can have a good room upstairs. Just as they are going to be taken up there the sounds of *samisen* and drums are heard from the apartments where Yuranosuke and his bevy of laughing girls are revelling. Kudayû draws Bannai's attention to the sounds and points out to him how Yuranosuke is carrying on. Bannai thinks that Yuranosuke must be crazy. He was sent here by his master Moronao, who though receiving several private letters from Kudayû,

could not believe that Yuranosuke was so far gone as that,
and ordered him to make inquiries and report at once if he
saw anything suspicious. But he is now convinced that
Kudayû was right. On this Kudayû says that he has
watched Yuranosuke so far but has not yet got to the
very bottom of his mind and he means to see it
through this evening. Talking thus on their way, they go
upstairs.

Meanwhile Yazama-Jûtaro, Senzaki-Yagorô, and Take-
mori-Kitahachi (Takebayashi-Tadashichi) followed by Tera-
oka Heiyemon (Terazaka-Kichiyemon) come up to the
tea-house through the wicket. After sending Heiyemon to
the servants' quarters to wait, they ask for admission. To
a waitress who has answered them, they state that they
desire to speak with Yuranosuke. They have sent messenger after messenger asking him to come to them, but
without success, and so they have come themselves to see
him and talk over matters.

The girl is afraid that they have taken the trouble for
nothing, for Master Yuranosuke has kept feasting and
drinking since the third of the month and is in such a
muddled state that it will be some time before he is himself
again. Yazama is astonished, but asks the girl to give him
the message all the same and sends her in.

Senzaki, too, expresses his amazement. He heard something of their chief's dissipation, but thought that it was
merely put on to throw the enemy off the scent. But now
their leader seems to have given himself up entirely to
pleasure, which is more than regrettable.

Takemori breaks in, saying that this shows that their
chief's spirit has completely changed. He thinks that the

best thing to do will be to rush in and slay him on the spot.

Yazama and Senzaki, however, are for having some talk with Yuranosuke first and then deciding what to do with him.

Just then Yuranosuke with his eyes bandaged appears, staggering towards where the three *rônin* are standing and surrounded by a number of girls with whom he is enacting the part of ' devil ' in a game of blindman's buff. The girls, shouting with laughter and clapping their hands, frolick about the drunken man, crying, " This way, devil ! This way where you hear our hands clapping ! "

Yuranosuke goes about here and there, saying that when he gets hold of one of them, he will make her swallow a good draught of *saké*. At last he seizes Yazama instead of a girl, calling for a *saké* pot to be brought at once.

Yazama disengaging himself announces his name as the bandage is taken off the eyes of Yuranosuke, and asks what all this buffoonery can mean. Yuranosuke confesses that he is done for, while the girls are clamouring that these great hulking fellows are spoiling all the fun.

Yazama now asks the girls to be good enough to leave Yuranosuke with them for a little while ; they have some matters to talk over with him.

Having thus dismissed them, the three men come near their chief who has lain on the mats in an apparent stupor and each, announcing his name, tries to wake him up. Yuranosuke, rising with a surprised air, bids them welcome and asks what they have come for. Yazama replies that they have come to learn when they are to start for Kamakura. As if this were a preposterous question,

Yuranosuke looks astonished and says that that is, indeed, a tremendously important matter; but apparently unable to think clearly about anything he muddles it with a line from an old ballad, bursts out singing a stanza of it, and then begs to be excused for talking foolishly.

The three men get angry and saying that they will do as they agreed if they cannot recall him to his senses, draw their swords and are going to fall upon their chief; when Heiyemon, who has just come on the scene, throws himself between them and his master and begs them to put up their weapons.

Teraoka-Heiyemon now addresses himself to Yuranosuke, who remembers him as a swift-footed common soldier sent northwards with letters some time ago. Heiyemon tells his chief how while up north he heard of the suicide of his lord and how he was beside himself with grief and rage, when on the way back the news reached him of the destruction of his lord's house and of the dispersion of the clan. He went to Kamakura and for three months lived there, dogging Moronao's movements in the hope of finding some opportunity of striking him, but in vain. As he came back to his parents' home in the country, he chanced to hear of a plot being set on foot to avenge his lord's death. So delighted at the news, he soon sought the gentlemen now with him at their inn and begged their assistance to get his name added to the list of confederates. And this evening he has followed them here to see the chief for that purpose.

On hearing this, Yuranosuke makes fun of him by saying that he is lighter of tongue than of foot and that he is really more fit to be a professional jester than anything else. As

for himself, he felt slightly indignant at first and formed a
league of some forty or fifty men to take vengeance, but
when he came to think of it, he found that if the plot failed,
his head would go off and if it succeeded, self-dispatch
would inevitably follow ; death either way.   Where would
be the use of seeking vengeance if he could not live to enjoy
it ? It would be like taking a decoction one moment and
getting strangled the next.   As for Heiyemon, he is but a
common soldier with a salary of five *ryô* and three men's
rations.   Considering his position, it seems rather funny
that he should trouble himself about his lord's mis-
fortunes.   And then if Heiyemon is bound to take one
head, Yuranosuke with his stipend of 1,500 *koku* ought
to take a bushel of heads at least.   That is too nonsensical,
so he has given it up.   It is far better to do as the rest of
the world.   Oh, the joyous note of the *samisen*, going *tsu-*
tsu-ten, tsu-tsu-ten ! There is nothing like making merry.

Heiyemon exclaims that his honour cannot be in earnest.
His pay was small enough, while his honour held a high
post, but they both drew their livelihood from one and the
same source and there is no difference in their gratitude to
their lord.   And though he knows that it is impudent for
a fellow of no worth like him to ask to be seen among the
great gentlemen of rank, he implores to be allowed to follow
them if only to tie their sandals or carry their burdens.
Saying so, Heiyemon prostrates himself before Yuranosuke,
but receiving no answer, he looks up, when he finds that
Yuranosuke has fallen asleep.

Takemori and the others notice this and thinking that
they have seen the real disposition of Yuranosuke, are
going to make an end of him as they have agreed as a

warning to their confederates. They lay their hands on their swords, but Heiyemon again interposes and restrains them from giving way to their anger. He says that if they will turn over the matter in their mind, they will see that Yuranosuke's conduct may be explained. Ever since their lord's death, he has encountered many difficulties in his wish to avenge it, while he has been compelled to bear in silence people's slanders. No one can know what anxieties he has had to pass through. Thus if he did not drink a bottle of *saké* now and then, he would be worn out with trouble and vexation. So Heiyemon begs them to wait till Yuranosuke wakes up, for then they will see him again in his right mind.

Thus advised the three *rônin* desist from their action and withdraw, accompanied by Heiyemon.

Now Yuranosuke's son Rikiya has been running all breathless from his home at Yamashina to this place. And peeping within he sees his father lying alone in a heavy sleep. Fearful of being heard by others, he comes quietly to his side and makes a slight clashing sound with his sword. Yuranosuke instantly gets up and seeing his son asks what has brought him here.

Rikiya hands him a letter from Lady Kaoyo just brought by an express messenger and says that their enemy Moronao has obtained permission to return to his province and in a few days will be ready to start. Details will be found in the letter.

Yuranosuke nods his acknowledgement and orders a palanquin to be sent for him in the night. The boy soon leaving, Yuranosuke, eager to learn the contents of the letter, is about to open it when Kudayû comes in, saying that he hopes he is not intruding upon him.

Concealing his vexation, Yuranosuke welcomes the visitor and noticing that the latter has grown somewhat older-looking than before, banters him by asking him if he is here to rub out the wrinkles in his forehead.

Kudayû sets himself at once to fathom Yuranosuke's mind, and citing the saying that he who does great things must be forgiven for trivail faults, says that he thinks Yuranosuke a fine man of great promise to begin his enterprise by idling in a tea-house, careless of men's blame. And he presses Yuranosuke to be frank with him and tell him that this dissipation of his is a mere blind to cover his revengeful designs against Moronao.

Yuranosuke flatly denies this though he professes himself obliged to Kudayû for the idea. He is really delighted that while he feared to be laughed at as a fool for hankering after girls when he is over forty years old, he should be taken as doing it all to cloak such a secret scheme as the other hints at.

And on being asked if he, then, does not really intend to avenge their lord's death, Yuranosuke assures Kudayû that he has no such intention whatever. When their lord's mansion and domain were confiscated, he spoke of dying on their own ground, but that was merely to please Lady Kaoyo. After Kudayû left them, saying that to fight with the government was the same as declaring oneself as a public enemy, they swaggered on but without coming to a decision. Then something was said of committing self-dispatch at their lord's tomb, but that, too, came to nothing and they stole out by the back gate. It is entirely owing to Kudayû's example that Yuranosuke is now anything but

wretched. So for old friendship's sake, he desires Kudayû
to be more at ease and have a draught together.

Kudayû agrees to this and they call for *saké* and begin
drinking, when he takes up a piece of octopus from a dish
beside him and offers it to Yuranosuke. As the latter
receives it with thanks and is about to eat it, Kudayû
reminds him of the fact that it is the eve of the anniversary
of their lord's death, which should be kept holy by abstaining from animal food, and asks him if he has the heart to
eat the fish without hesitation. Yuranosuke immediately
answers that he has, for he has not heard that Lord Enya
has turned into an octopus after his death. It was, indeed,
his stupidity that made them both *rônin*. They have good
reason to detest his memory. He may bear him grudge,
but he is not in the least to fast on his account. Saying so
he eats it at a mouthful, causing such astonishment to the
crafty Kudayû that he cannot utter a word.

Yuranosuke then says that it is ill eating after all. They
cannot drink with such poor food. They will have a
fowl killed and broiled. And he invites his friend to go
within and hear the women sing while they drink. With
this he rises and affecting a drunken gait, leads the way to
the inner apartment.

Kudayû, however, does not follow him and remains
behind, looking at Yuranosuke as he goes staggering away,
when Sagisaka-Bannai, who has been secretly watching him,
comes in and joins Kudayû. Bannai says that from one
who does not refrain from animal food on the eve of the
anniversary of his master's death, revenge is not to be
expected. He will inform Moronao of this and end his
anxiety.

Kudayû agrees with Bannai, saying that there seems to be no longer any need for guard. And pointing to the sword left by Yuranosuke, he adds that to forget thus the soul of a samurai proves that he is no better than a spiritless brute, and the rustiness of the blade, which ought to be kept bright, shows still more clearly the rottenness of the man's character so that they need trouble themselves about him no further.

They are now for going away, and order Kudayû's palanquin to be brought to the verandah. When it comes, Kudayû makes as if to enter it but deftly conceals himself under the verandah.

Without knowing this, Bannai speaks of Kampei's wife O-Karu being in the house and asks Kudayû if he knows her. Surprised at receiving no answer, he lifts the hanging screen of the palanquin and, looking in, is astonished to see there nothing but a stepping-stone. He wonders if Kudayû has met the fate of Sayohime of Matsura.[1] As he looks round with a perplexed air, he hears himself spoken to by Kudayû from under the verandah.

Kudayû tells Bannai that he has slipped out of the palanquin in order to find out somehow or other the contents of the letter brought by Rikiya to his father, because he feels somewhat uneasy about it. He will let Bannai know as soon as he succeeds in doing so, so he desires him to accompany the palanquin as if he were in it. And Bannai does as requested.

Meanwhile O-Karu appears at the balustrade of the upper

---

[1] The legend runs that when her lord Satehiko left on an expedition to Korea, Sayohime stood on a hill on the shore of Matsura and waved her scarf to his vessel. She stood there so long that she was finally turned into a stone.

verandah, breathing the fresh air to dispel the effects of
the *saké* she has been drinking.   She is already used to her
new life and is cheering her spirits in the cool breeze.
Soon Yuranosuke comes to her and says that he is just
going to fetch his precious sword that he has forgotten
downstairs, and wishes her to tidy the room a little while
he is away.

Re-entering the room where he had his conversation with
Kudayû, Yuranosuke is surprised to find the latter gone.
He looks round to make sure that he is alone and approaching the hanging lantern above the verandah, reads Lady
Kaoyo's letter by its light.   As it is a pretty long letter
written on a scroll of paper with many redundant phrases
such as women love to use, he is taking time in wading
through it.   O-Karu, who is looking down from above,
thinking with envy that it may be a letter from some
sweetheart, leans over the balustrade in the vain attempt to
make out what it is about.   She thinks of her metal minor,
and bringing it manages to read the letter by its reflection.

Meanwhile Kudayû, who has all this time lain concealed
under the verandah, sees one end of the letter coming down
to the ground and continues to read it by the help of the
moonlight.   He further manages to tear off a portion which
he intends to keep as a proof.

Just then O-Karu's hairpin comes loose and falls on a
stone below.   Startled by the noise, Yuranosuke looks
suddenly up, instinctively hiding the letter behind him.
A cunning smile crosses Kudayû's face, while O-Karu,
confused at being detected, hastily shuts up her mirror.

A sudden idea comes into Yuranosuke's head, and calling
to O-Karu he asks her to come down ; he says that he has

something to tell her. O-Karu consents and is about to
come round by the stairs, when Yuranosuke, finding a
small ladder close by and leaning it against the eaves,
tells her to come down by it.   For some reason he does not
wish her to meet anybody on the way.   When with some
difficulty she comes down the ladder to him, Yuranosuke
asks her if she saw anything from up where she was.   She
hesitates to answer, but when pressed closely, she says that
she saw him looking much pleased with a letter.   Then
he says that she must have read the whole of it.   O-Karu
does not confess to it, but Yuranosuke is quite sure that she
did and shows his vexation.   On her asking him what is
annoying him, he says that he loves her so much that he
wants her to be his wife.   Such a sudden proposal cannot
be taken seriously by the woman, but on Yuranosuke's
saying that he will redeem her this very evening and after
keeping her by his side for three days he will set her free to
join her lover or go to her parents, O-Karu shows her great
delight but still fears that he is only joking with her.   On
this Yuranosuke tells her that he will see the proprietor
of the house and make arrangements at once and desires
her to stay quietly where she is for a little time until he
returns.   The last point is very important, he says, and so
she must observe it to the letter.

O-Karu is overjoyed at the prospect held out to her and
loading Yuranosuke with thanks as he hastens away to fulfil
his promise, stays behind as requested.
A song is heard within.

> " If ever was a hapless maid,
>   That I am for certain;
> For days and days I wait and pine

For my dearest lover ;
    With stifled sighs I lie and mourn,
        Like a lonely plover."

Feeling how well the song fits her own position, O-Karu
is deep in thought, when she is surprised by the unlooked-
for appearance of her brother Heiyemon.   She is ashamed
to be seen by him in this place and covers her face with her
hands.   But Heiyemon tells her that he has heard everything from their mother and thinks that she has acted nobly
in thus sacrificing herself for her husband's sake, that is,
in their lord's service.   At this O-Karu feels happy again,
and tells him what will, she thinks, gladden him too.   She
is going to be redeemed, unexpectedly, by Ôboshi-Yuranosuke, who will afterwards allow her to join her husband.

This is news to Heiyemon.   He does not know why
Yuranosuke is going to do so.   It may be that Yuranosuke
knows O-Karu to be the wife of Kampei and is going to
redeem her for his sake.   But on being told that Yuranosuke knows nothing of it, Heiyemon cannot but imagine
him to be a libertine to the core.   And it looks very much
to him as if Yuranosuke had no wish any more to avenge
his lord.

O-Karu, however, assures her brother that he is wrong
and whispers to him the contents of the letter she has read.
Heiyemon is surprised and making sure of the fact that the
proposal of Yuranosuke was made after she had read the
letter, says that she cannot now escape death.   And telling
her that he must decide her fate, all of a sudden he draws
his sword and strikes at her.

Springing aside, O-Karu asks him what wrong she has
done.   She has her husband and parents and if she has done

wrong, they should punish her, not Heiyemon. Now that
Yuranosuke is going to redeem her, she will soon see them.
She is feeling so happy, and so whatever she may have done,
she asks her brother to pardon her.

She clasps her hands to him in entreaty. Heiyemon,
filled with pity for his poor sister who knows nothing about
her father and husband, flings his sword away and shedding
tears tells her that their father Yoichibei was murdered by
a highwayman on the night just before she left her home
and that Kampei, whom she hopes soon to rejoin, took
his own life on the day of her departure. The news is too
much for her and she faints. On coming to, she clings
to her brother's arm and cries her heart out.

O-Karu wants to know why her husband died, but as
it would take too long to tell in full, Heiyemon does not
go into details. He only tells her how their poor mother
was beside herself with grief and how she begged him not
to say anything about it to O-Karu lest she should weep
herself to death at the terrible news. And he should
indeed have kept silent if he had not learnt what she has
done. Yuranosuke has no cause to redeem her if he does
not know she is Kampei's wife, and on the other hand he
is certainly not infatuated with love for her. The letter
she read contains a matter of great importance, and it is
quite clear that he means to put her to death to keep his
secret when he has redeemed her. Even if she does not
tell of the letter, walls have ears, as they say ; and if the
contents were to get abroad, it would be attributed to her.
She was wrong to peep into a secret letter ; she must be
killed. It is better then to die by her brother's hand than
by that of some other man. And if Heiyemon slays his

sister as a woman who has knowledge of the great plot,. Yuranosuke will let him join the leaguers and accompany them to Kamakura. The lot of a man of low estate is sad, indeed, for unless Heiyemon shows himself superior in spirit to others, he cannot hope to be allowed to take part in their chief's undertaking. On that account, he askes her to give him her life.

The unfortunate woman, sobbing and sobbing all the time, cannot at first make any reply. At last, mastering her emotion, she laments deeply for her father and hus- band, especially for her husband who was hardly thirty years of age. She is overwhelmed with grief that she cannot see him again. She has now nothing to live for and can die at any moment. Only she must not die by her brother's hand, or their mother will be angry with him. So she will kill herself and afterwards if her head or body be of service to her brother, he is free to make use of it. And bidding him farewell, she takes up his sword and places the point against her throat.

At this crisis Yuranosuke suddenly comes upon the scene. Perceiving how matters are, he hastily catches. O-Karu's arm and stops her. She cries out to him to let her die, while her brother is startled at the unlooked-for appearance of his chief.

Yuranosuke quietly speaks to them, saying that the brother and sister have cleared all doubts of them from his mind. Heiyemon shall accompany him to the East, while O-Karu shall live on and duly mourn the dead.

O-Karu, however, would rather accompany her loved ones to the other world than mourn them. But Yurano- suke, keeping a firm hold on the sword, says that though

her husband Kampei has joined the league, he has not had
the luck to kill a single enemy and will have no plea to
make when he meets his lord in the other world. She
has now an opportunity to provide that plea for him.

So saying, Yuranosuke thrusts the sword which O-
Karu still holds between the mats through the floor, piercing a man, who has been lying hidden under there, through
his shoulder. He orders Heiyemon to drag the fellow
out. Instantly Heiyemon jumps off the verandah and
pulling him roughly out, is surprised to find that the
wretch is Kudayû. He throws the man at the feet of Yuranosuke, who catches him by the hair and vituperates him as
the worm that feeds in the lion's belly. He was rewarded
well by his lord while alive and honoured with his special
favour, and yet he has become the sleuth-hound of his
murderer Moronao, secretly informing the enemy of their
clan of everything he could get wind of. Forty and more
of those under Yuranosuke have left their parents, parted
from their families, or sent their wives who should be
their life-long partners to lead a life of shame, all to avenge
their lord. Waking or dreaming they ponder over the
circumstances of their lord's death with their bowels
twisted with grief. Especially this evening, of all others
the very eve of the anniversary of their lord's death, when
they should keep it holy by abstaining from all unclean
food—and Yuranosuke has endeavoured to do so though
he was forced to say reluctantly some irreverent things
about his lord—Kudayû dared to thrust the flesh of fish
to his face. Great was Yuranosuke's agony when he could
not accept and yet dared not refuse it. And it may be
imagined with what shame and anguish he let it go down

his throat, he whose family for three generations has
served the house of Lord Enya.   His whole body seemed
all at once go to pieces for this horrible act.   Kudayû is,.
indeed, the devil, a hound of hell.

With these words Yuranosuke presses Kudayû's head
down on the ground.   And ordering Heiyemon to bring
his sword, he tells him to cut Kudayû about.   On account
of its rustiness, the gashes made are all only a few inches
long.   He strikes Kudayû till he is covered with wounds,
when Yuranosuke bethinking himself says that it might
be awkward if they killed the fellow in the garden, and tells
Heiyemon to take him away as if he were simply dead-
drunk.   And he throws his *haori* upon the half-dead man
so as to cover his wounds.

At this juncture, the partition is suddenly pushed back
and Yazama, Senzaki, and Takemori, who have been
listening in secret, come in and apologize humbly to
Yuranosuke for their conduct.

Yuranosuke, paying no head to them, orders Heiyemon
to take the drunken guest to the River Kamo and give him
a bellyful of water gruel.

The predominant note of this great act is one of gaiety,
making on the one hand an agreeable contrast with the two
preceding gloomy acts and forming on the other a breathing space in the play, after which it soon gains in seriousness and quickens its tragic steps to the end.   The laying
of the scene at a tea-house, which is merry with girls'
laughter and the music of the *samisen*, upholds this note as
nothing else could and helps to envelop everything in the
comic spirit which is sustained admirably throughout.

The comedy here is interwoven with some tragic threads ; they are not, however, brought to their fruition, but are agreeably settled or dealt with lightly in accordance with the ruling spirit.

Of the three comic episodes in the act, the first is that between Kudayû and Yuranosuke. Kudayû with his son is dealt with in the fourth act only slightly, scarcely enough to bring out his meanness, but the audience is supplied with historial facts sufficient to brand him as a reptile, and hates him before he does anything on the stage. The authors, however, have made a hit in bringing him in as a spy for one who should be his enemy. His way of testing Yuranosuke by offering him a piece of fish on the eve of the anniversary of Yenya's death may appear trifling to Westerners, but for a Japanese who has been taught to refrain from animal food on such an occasion, to take it is a crime against one's conscience, almost tantamount to breaking one of the ten commandments. So cruel is the test that to dare it even for the sake of keeping up the deception excites the sympathy of the audience, making the final discomfiture of Kudayû all the more gratifying. Everything is managed skilfully. Yuranosuke knows from the loss of a part of the letter that Kudayû is under the floor, so he tells O-Karu never to leave the room, thereby depriving Kudayû of any chance of escape. It is natural for Kudayû to try to eavesdrop while he is near and so to come just under Yuranosuke, that he may hear more easily. His ear is most probably pressed against the floor. All this leads him to his ultimate ruin. Kudayû is nearly killed but not completely, in order not to transgress the bounds of tragedy. The last touch seen in the order to give water gruel to Kudayû is light enough to turn his end into something laughable.

The second comic thread is the visit of the three *rônin* coming to sound Yuranosuke as to his intention of carrying out their plot. This is based on the fact that Ôishi's debauchery to put his enemy off the scent was so thorough than even his confederates grew doubtful of his intentions and came to see him one after another at tea-houses. And it is used here to show off by contrast Yuranosuke's disgusting foolei . The situation is very much strained in the first part, but it is readily set right in connection with another thread and Yuranosuke's paying no attention to the apology of the *rônin*, which shows how lightly he looks on their meddling, is a happy way of ending this piece of comedy.

The remaining comic thread is that of O-Karu and Heiyemon. Heiyemon standing for Terazaki-Kichiyemon, who was not related to O-Karu in reality, is a favourite character with the populace, for he, like Terazaki, is not of the samurai class but of a grade lower, and yet aspires to be loyal to his master. Heiyemon's reasoning with his sister to let him take her life appears to be too cold-blooded and ferociously selfish to modern people, but if she must die, it would be far better for her to end her life at the hand of one she loves than at another's. And, indeed, for Heiyemon nothing short of such a sacrifice would be enough to prove his fidelity to his chief and his worthiness to join the cause. At this moment O-Karu's proposal to kill herself is very appropriate : it would save her brother from the sin of fratricide while atoning amply for her inexcusable fault. What would end in tragedy, however, is happily turned into comedy by the appearance of Yuranosuke, who recognizes the sincerity of brother and sister and stops her from committing useless suicide. The end of this thread is cleverly interlaced with those of the other two, bringing each to a satisfactory settlement.

The central figure in the act is, of course, Yuranosuke, whose character is finely delineated. He is reppresented as given up to pleasures and drunkenness to befool his spies, refusing to come to his senses even before his confederates. But that he is wariness itself even in his drunkenness is shown in his waking up at once at the slight clashing of a sword. This touch has been suggested by the saying, " At clang of bridle-ring the sleeping hero wakes," and paints him as a samurai to the bone. And then his systematic keeping on his mask before his enemy even under a severe trial argues him to be ever on the alert. So when he feels safe he not only sobers up at once but shows himself mindful of his duty and ready to act properly in any circumstances. And we are acquainted with his true mind even before hearing his strong language against Kudayû, the language which goes straight into the hearts of his listeners and thrills them to the marrow.

Act VIII.   THE BRIDAL JOURNEY

It will be remembered that in the second act Rikiya, the son of Yuranosuke, is shown as affianced to Konami, the daughter of Honzô. Honzô, the councillor of Sir Wakasano-suke, is doing well in Kamakura, while Yuranosuke, since the destruction of the house of his lord, Enya, has with-drawn to Yamashina near Kyoto and is living in obscurity. Thus though still linked with him by love, Konami is left deserted by Rikiya without their enagagement having been confirmed by the customary exchange of betrothal presents. She is given to moody thoughts, so her mother Tonasé resolves to take her to Yuranosuke's place and give her in marriage to her lover Rikiya. This act gives a description of their long journey on foot from Kamakura to Yamashina.

Though mainly in the form of a dialogue, the description is metrical and is intended not to be acted but sung or recited by a group of accompanists, the actors only following the words with appropriate gestures so arranged as to form a kind of continuous slow dance.

This form of arrangement is peculiar to the Japanese classical drama known as *kabuki* and is considered inseparable from it. It was retained as a relic of the puppet play by the influence of which the classical drama was developed. In the puppet-play, all dialogues were, of course, carried on by accompanists, who further described actions or expressed incidental sentiments in verse. These descriptive or emotional portions were interspersed through the whole of a play much in the manner of choruses in the Greek drama. And as if not content with mere interspersions, it was a rule to devote the whole of one act to a lyrical interlude. This is known as *michiyuki* or progress scene, for it has for its theme a journey taken by some of the characters, and a desciption of the changing scenery on the road is given with the sentiments aroused from time to time in the characters, showing the state of their minds as they proceed towards a certain action they have in view.

In the present *michiyuki*, Konami regrets that fortune has never smiled on her, but as she goes on, though her

Plate IV.   A charming scene in the bridal journey (Act VIII).

Plate IV. A charming scene in the bridal journey (Act VIII).

fate will be like a white cloud vanishing from Mt. Fuji, she hopes that her sadness will be charmed away by the bonfire to be lighted at her wedding. Presently they see the bridal train of some daimyô's daughter going through an avenue of pine-trees at Miho, and Konami envies its grand state, for so she herself might have travelled for her marriage if the times had not changed. Her mother tries to cheer her spirits as they pass Fuchû (Shizuoka) with a picture of her daughter's wedding ceremony. On crossing the Ôi River, Konami is reminded of the saying that current of a stream and a man's heart are alike fickle things. But she does not fear her lover's heart. Only she is afraid that under the ban of misfortune their love's full flower may hardly blow. So they travel on, Konami chased by fear after fear which her mother strives to drive away till they arrive at their journey's end.

It is rather difficult to stage such an interlude, for the scene has to be shifted from time to time. So usually two or three prominent scenes are selected for convenience and the rest are left to be supplied from imagination. And then as two characters only—the principal characters are mostly two in number in such a scene—are too few to sustain interest for long, so recourse is usually had to some means of breaking the monotony. In the present *michi-yuki*, the bridal train is introduced for this purpose, and then after that a pack-horse woman, palanquin-bearers, Isé pilgrims, and others are brought in here and there. But at any rate as the scene is not tediously long, on the whole it does well for a change.

Act IX. THE REPENTANCE OF HONZÔ

The scene is laid in the house of Ôboshi-Yuranosuke in the village of Yamashina. One of the rooms comes right to the edge of the stage with another at the back, partitioned off with sliding-screens. On the left a verandah goes up a little way, which is joined to a short open corridor leading to the entrance of the house. Beyond the verandah and corridor is seen the front yard with a gate and a bamboo bush, all now covered heavily with snow.

It is morning and Yuranosuke has come home from the tea-house in Gion-machi where he has been kept for the night by the snow. He is attended by some jesters and waitresses from the tea-house, and being still under the influence of *saké*, on entering the yard, he falls to rolling the snow up into a big ball, in which attempt he himself rolls in the snow instead of rolling it up, much to the merriment of his attendants.

While his attendants are with him, he speaks of the attractions of Gion-machi, depreciating his own humble dwelling and acting rudely to his wife O-Ishi (O-Riku) who has appeared to welcome him home.

As he falls prostrate and goes to sleep in entering the room, O-Ishi thanks the attendants for their trouble and sends them back. But no sooner are they out of hearing than Yuranosuke gets up and asks his son Rikiya in a sober tone the meaning of his rolling up the snow which he pretended that he did for fun. Rikiya thinks that snow is so light that it is easily blown away by the least breeze, but that when it is pressed into a big ball, it gets so hard that by rolling down a hillside it may crush even huge rocks. So is the force of their united loyalty under the pressure of affliction. But neither the united loyalty nor the ball of snow must be kept too long. Rikiya asks his father if he has read his mind aright.

Yuranosuke, however, was not thinking of that. The forty-seven confederates, Yuranosuke, his son, Hara, and the rest, are all masterless men, living in the shade. In the shade that mass of snow would take long enough to melt. It teaches them to persevere to assure success. Haste makes waste, as they say ; in the meantime, however, they will do the best they can. And ordering the ball of snow to be taken into the small shaded court at the back to keep it from melting, he withdraws to the adjoining room to write letters.

Presently a woman visitor comes to the house. She makes the palanquin which has come with her wait outside, and alone, girding on two swords like a man and strict in deportment, demands admission at the door. To a woman-servant who has answered the call, she announces herself as Tonasé, the wife of Kakogawa-Honzô, who has come a great distance in the hope of being allowed an interview with Master Ôboshi-Yuranosuke. Then she calls her daughter Konami, who steps out of the palanquin, gladsome to be at her lover's home as a bush-warbler at sight of a plum-tree all aflower.

When they are shown in, Konami keeps close to her mother and sits bashfully beside her, and the next moment O-Ishi enters with a graceful step to meet them.

O-Ishi welcomes her guests and says that she ought long since to have called but for the situation she is in, and that their attention makes her feel quite ashamed of herself.

Tonasé asks her not to make such strangers of them.   It is true that they meet each other for the first time, but since Master Rikiya and Konami were betrothed, they are both of them mothers-in-law and she is sure that they need not stand upon ceremony with each other.   And she proceeds to say that after the betrothal of their children, an unexpected turn took place in the fortunes of Lord Enya and they could not discover where Master Rikiya, together with his father, dwelt.   Such changes are common enough in this world but unchangeable is the heart of her husband.   At last they found that Master Yuranosuke and his family were living here at Yamashina, and in their desire to make over their daughter to them as soon as possible, she has brought her for a visit this day.   Her husband Honzô should have come, but as he could not, he gave her his two swords which she now carries in her girdle to represent him, so she is here now as his deputy.   She desires to see Master Yuranosuke to talk over the matter and to have the marriage consummated.

O-Ishi, however, says that these words are quite unexpected to her.   Her husband is away from home just now and cannot answer himself, but everything has changed since the time of their children's betrothal.   Yuranosuke is now only a *rônin* without a single follower, while Master Honzô is high in his lord's service.   Their children's marriage would be, as the vulgar saying goes, as ill-matched as a lantern and a temple-bell.   Besides the betrothal has not been confirmed by the customary exchange of bridal presents, and so her husband says that it will be no slight to them if Konami should find another bridegroom.

Tonasé is surprised at these words. However much O-Ishi may humble herself, she cannot say that it is an ill match between the two houses. When the betrothal was made, Master Yuranosuke had an appointment worth 1,500 *koku*, while Honzô was allotted as now 500 *koku* by the year, that is 1,000 *koku* less. And though now Master Yuranosuke, compelled by misfortune to become a *rônin*, gets no stipend, he is only less than Honzô by 500 *koku*.

O-Ishi answers Tonasé by saying that the difference of 500, or even 1,000, *koku* would not really matter, if only Master Honzô did not differ so much from her husband in disposition.

This Tonasé cannot understand. She asks O-Ishi how that is so ; when the latter replies that though her master Lord Enya's death was due to his hasty temper, it originated in his refusal to dishonour himself by offering bribes. And his retainers honoured him for that. But Master Honzô, though a samurai, stooped to cajole Moronao with a bribe. There's the rub, and Yuranosuke cannot receive the daughter of such a man as a bride for his son.

Tonasé instantly shuffles forward, taking offence at O-Ishi's words. She says that though she cannot pocket the insult under ordinary circumstances, for her daughter's sake, she will pass it over, for the side of the wife must always give way to that of the husband. But whether the marriage ceremony has taken place or not, her daughter is the wife of Master Rikiya before all the world.

O-Ishi pooh-poohs it all as but fine talk. At all events if Konami is her son's wife, he divorces her ; O-Ishi divorces her in her son's name. So saying she stands up and push-ing back the partition disappears.

The girl bursts out crying. She has come here with her mother fully expecting to be united to Rikiya whom she loves so much, and never imagining she would be thus cruelly driven away by her mother-in-law. She entreats her mother to plead for her and prevent her marriage from being broken off.

Tonasé gazes upon her daughter wistfully. It may be a parent's partiality, she says, but her daughter appears to possess more beauty than any other ten girls put together ; and so she looked for a good husband for her and betrothed her to Rikiya. She is extremely sorry that their journey here has been in vain. But she cannot understand very well why Konami is put away so easily. Perhaps it is that being *rônin* they are now at their wits' end to support themselves and so have hit upon marrying their son to some rich merchant's daughter with an eye to money. When such people reject her daughter, she can throw the insult back in their faces. There are plenty of families who will be glad to receive Konami as a bride. There is no reason why she should not marry elsewhere. So Tonasé urges her daughter to answer firmly without weeping.

It has taken some time for Konami to master herself. At last she upbraids her mother for saying such cruel things. When she left home, her father told her that she was most fortunate in meeting with such a husband as Rikiya, who, *rônin* as he is, is of excellent parts. Since a virtuous woman never looks upon a second husband, she was not, even if she parted from him, to take another one. Above all, sleeping or waking she was not to forget to be tender to her husband and dutiful to her parents-in-law. She was not to show a jealous disposition even by way of a joke. She remember her father's very words. If she is put away, she cannot help it, but she will not add grief upon grief to her father by becoming the wife of anyone but Rikiya.

On hearing Konami's determination to persist in her love, Tonasé is unable to contain her emotion and overcome with tears, she draws her sword. The girl, surprised, restrains her. The mother says that when she thinks with what pleasure her father is looking forward to the marriage, she cannot take her daughter home even if she is driven away. Especially as Konami is not her own, but his former wife's daughter, he may think that Tonasé has failed to do all she might in bringing about the marriage, like all step-mothers who are proverbially careless about their step-children. She cannot go home alive. When she is dead, Konami will tell her father why her mother has sought death.

Konami, however, cannot allow this. She says that it is not her mother but she who is hated by her husband that ought to die. Alive she is but a trouble to both her father and mother and causes them nothing but grief. She beseeches her mother to take her life. She would fain die on the threshold of the house from which she is driven away.

Tonasé sees the justness of Konami's words, but her daughter shall not die alone. She will do as her daughter asks her to, but she will not be long after the girl. She bids her to be ready and, restraining her tears, prepares to give the fatal stroke.

Just then the shrill notes of a pipe are heard outside. An itinerant minstrel is playing the air of the " Nesting of the

Crane." Tonasé reflects that, though a bird, the crane
loves her young. But what a terrible fate is hers that she
should have to take the life of her innocent child ! Distract-
ed with grief, she can with difficulty stand firm, while she
raises the blade aloft, under which Konami kneels down
bravely with her hands joined in prayer. But before she
strikes, a voice calls out loudly, " Forbear ! "

Astonished at this unexpected interruption, Tonasé looks
round irresolutely. As her grasp on the fatal weapon
relaxes, the sound of the pipe ceases. She thinks that the
minstrel is being sent away by the voice. She secretly
wishes that some help would come to them, but hating to be
laughed at for faltering, she raises the weapon a second time.
As she does so, again the pipe is played and again the voice
calls out, " Forbear ! "

Tonasé is perplexed and wonders whether the voice is
to send the minstrel away with a gift or to stay her hand.

" It is to stay your hand," exclaims O-Ishi's voice from
within ; " my son Rikiya shall marry your daughter."

Nothing could have at once astonished and gladdened
Tonasé more than this, and while she asks if this is true,
singing a snatch from the wedding song in her joy :

> " O the pine-trees twain,
> Like years, like love attain ! "

O-Ishi appears, carrying a small stand of plain wood on
a level with her eyes. Setting it before Tonasé, she expresses
her admiration for Tonasé's resoluteness to take the life of
her daughter and also for Konami's chastity of heart. This
marriage, she says, distasteful though it is to her, shall take
place. In return, however, she expects a bridal gift which
is not commonly given to be placed on the stand.

Tonasé feels greatly relieved and returns her drawn sword to its scabbard. She is most willing to satisfy O-Ishi's desire. The pair of swords she carries with her are heirlooms in her husband's family. They were made by two celebrated swordsmiths and there is nothing her husband values more highly. These she asks her to accept.

But O-Ishi will take nothing of the kind. She wants to have the head of Kakogawa-Honzô placed on the stand !

The request is so preposterous that it strikes both mother and child speechless. But Tonasé cannot remain long without asking O-Ishi why. The latter answers that when their Lord Enya, having a grudge against Moronao, attacked him with his sword in the palace at Kamakura, it was solely because Kakogawa-Honzô, who as luck would have it was present, caught him from behind and stopped him that his enemy got off with no more than slight wounds, while he himself was compelled to commit self-dispatch without satisfying his wrath. Though no word of it passed his lips, they well knew how great was his mortification and how intense was his hatred for Master Honzô. They are still liegemen of their ill-fated chief ; and if Tonasé would that the daughter of Honzô become the wife of Rikiya, she must present them with her husband's head on the stand. As soon as this is done, the marriage shall take place without further delay.

At these sharp words of inexorable logic, mother and child hang their heads and are at a loss what to do, when a voice from outside is heard, exclaiming that the head of Kakogawa-Honzô is willingly offered. And the minstrel who has been standing at the door comes in and taking off his deep-brimmed hat, reveals the features of Honzô.

Tonasé and Konami are astonished and ask him what has brought him here in such a disguise.

Honzō says in answer that he has heard all that has passed. He came here secretly for a special purpose of which he will tell Tonasé more later. And turning to O-Ishi, he says that he has the honour of addressing the wife of Master Yuranosuke. He foresaw that matters would take this turn and came, without telling his wife, to find out for himself. As he expected, his head is desired as a bridal gift. But that is what a true samurai should say. Yuranosuke, lost in dissipation and enervated with excessive drinking, has quite given up the idea of avenging his chief's death, a perfect model of a spiritless lout. And as a frog's offspring can but become a frog, Rikiya must be an idot no less than his father. Honzô's neck is in no danger from the blunt-edged swords of such good-for-nothing samurai as they. He does not want any more of such nonsense. And setting his foot on the stand and crushing it to pieces, he says that it is he who will not have Rikiya for his son-in-law.

O-Ishi cannot bear such insolence. She says that she will show him if the rusty weapon of a *rônin* has an edge or not. Unworthy as she is, she is the wife of Yuranosuke and is willing to try her skill with him. Saying so she gathers up her dress and taking down a spear from the wall, is going to attack Honzô.

At this sight Tonasé and Konami are startled and throw themselves on Honzô, who pushes them aside with an angry exclamation. And as O-Ishi makes a hurried thrust at him, he seizes the spear by the socket and twists it away from his body. On a second thrust he kicks the spear and

sends it into the air ; and without troubling himself any
more about the weapon, he seizes O-Ishi by the girdle and
throws her down on the mat.   He then sets his knee upon
her, while she gnashes her teeth with mortification.

As the mother and daughter are looking on in fear and
distress, Rikiya unexpectedly rushes in and taking up the
fallen spear, thrusts it in at Honzô's chest.   The latter
utters a deep groan and falls heavily on his face, while his
wife and daughter cling to him with grief and horror.

At this moment Yuranosuke suddenly comes upon the
scene and telling Rikiya to stop and saluting the wounded
man, says that Honzô must be satisfied to have fallen by the
hand of his son-in-law as he most desired.

Seeing that Yuranosuke has divined his real wishes,
Honzô opens his eyes and says that he understood Yuranosuke's great anxiety to avenge his lord's death and his
seeming dissipation to throw his enemy off his guard.   He
must have collected many confederates together.   As
Honzô thinks of it, he should have acted as Yuranosuke is
acting now.   A year ago his master Wakasanosuke was so
strongly determined to avenge the insult given him by
Moronao at the inauguration at Tsurugaoka that Honzô
saw no way of averting the peril except by shamelessly
bribing Moronao to change his attitude towards Wakasanosuke.   Honzô succeeded in it, but at the same time his
act resulted in aggravating Moronao's anger towards Lord
Enya.   That day he caught Lord Enya from behind because he thought that by doing so he might render the
latter's self-dispatch unnecessary.   In that he erred griev-
ously, and since that time he has never ceased to repent the
fault he then committed.   His daughter's present trouble is,

indeed, one of the consequences of his error. As an
atonement he has travelled here to offer his grey head to his
son-in-law. Sending his wife and daughter on in advance,
he came here by a different route two days before them.
The playing on the pipe he learnt in his youth was useful to
him, and lurking about the neighbourhood for four days,
he saw clearly what were Yuranosuke's intentions. It then
seemed to him that, if he fell by Yuranosuke's hand, the
latter's hatred of Honzô would cease and he would
consent to the union of Konami with Rikiya. If that hope
should be realized, he would be infinitely grateful. His
life, which he thought not to give up except in his master's
cause, he now yields for his child's sake. He asks Yuranosuke to take it and comply with the last prayer of a
father.

Choked with his tears, the wounded man can utter nothing
more, while his wife and daughter are beside themselves
with grief.

Yuranosuke says to Honzô that no doubt the latter feels
resentment at their not taking marriage and grudge separately. But there is a deep reason for that. And as Honzô is not long for this world, he will lay bare to him his
most secret thought.

So saying Yuranosuke pushes back the sliding-doors
which open to the inner court and displays to the dying
man's view two five-storied tombs of snow which he has
made to show what the final result of his designs will surely be.

Tonasé at once comprehends him. When Yuranosuke
has avenged his lord's death, she says, he will melt away
like the snow without serving another master. Master

Rikiya, too, has sought to put away her daughter, not from harshness, but out of pity. She grieves to think of the ill-will she bore O-Ishi.

O-Ishi admits that Tonasé speaks truly. To receive a bride merely that she shall so soon become a widow is too cruel to think of. It was because she did not wish for such a wedding that she spoke so harshly and unfeelingly to Tonasé.

It is now Tonasé's turn to apologize for her unwarranted guess that Rikiya, lost to all sense of shame and justice, was planning to become a rich merchant's son-in-law. She is so sorry and ashamed of it that she can hardly lift her eyes to O-Ishi.

Konami, O-Ishi avers, in birth and beauty is all that they could desire as a bride for their son. But she feels very pitiful for her that she has been born so unfortunate.

Here Honzô, mastering his emotion, expresses his joy at having his wish fulfilled. He extols Yuranosuke for his unparalleled fidelity and says that in becoming the wife of Rikiya, the worthy son of so unique a father, his daughter is a hundred times more fortunate than if she had married into the nobility. To the husband of his most honoured daughter he would like to make bridal gifts. So saying the dying man draws a folded paper from his bosom and gives it to Rikiya.

Rikiya receives it with a bow and opening it with his father is astonished to find it not a list of gifts but a detailed plan of Moronao's mansion. Yuranosuke knows not how to thank him, for it is the very thing he was wanting to get. For some time past all preparations have been made, but for lack of a guide like that they could not advance a step in their enterprise. As they have arranged to make an attack by night, they will get over the wall by scaling ladders and, forcing open the rain-shutters, then rush in and make their way to their enemy's apartments . . . .

So father and son, rejoicing, talk over their plans as if they were actually on the spot already; when Honzô, in spite of his pain, cautions them against making mistakes from over-confidence. Moronao, he says, keeps strict guard. All his sliding-doors are furnished with fastenings and his rain-shutters are bolted and barred so that they cannot be prized open, while to break them down with mallets would make far too much noise.

Yuranosuke, however, has provided for that. He has taken a hint from the bamboos in his yard, which, now bending under their load of snow, will resume their natural position as soon as the weight is taken off. He will procure a number of bamboo bows and, applying their ends between the lintel and the sill, cut their strings all at once; and, by applying the force with which they suddenly straighten themselves, he will make all the shutters come off the groove and fall down.

The wounded man, delighted with this device, forgets his condition for a moment. Rikiya now suggests that as, by the kindness of Honzô, they are in possession of the plan of their enemy's mansion, he will go down to the merchant, Amagawaya-Gihei at the port of Sakai and make arrangements for their equipment.

Yuranosuke's plan is different. As everybody knows that he is living at Yamashina, he cannot muster all his confederates at his place. He will go himself at once to Sakai and wait for all the rest to come, when they will start from there together. Meanwhile Rikiya, with his mother, bride, and her parents, remains behind and sees that nothing goes wrong. He will have this night to himself and can follow his father by boat later.

And saying that Honzô's disguise will be very useful to him, Yuranosuke puts on the robe and deep-brimmed wicker-hat, which turn him into an itinerant minstrel. In gratitude to Honzô and to dispel his anxiety in the other world, he allows this one night of love to the young couple. And as he prepares to depart, whistling on his pipe, O-Ishi, her heart filled with unutterable grief, wishes him a successful issue to his enterprise.

Honzô is rapidly sinking and cannot answer any more the cries of his daughter. Overwhelmed with grief, the widow and orphan kneel by the corpse and begin reciting the prayers for the dead. The sound of departing foot-steps ceases awhile and the Requiem is heard played on the pipe.

The incidents in this act were mostly taken from other plays, especially from Chikamatsu's *Goban-Taiheiki*, the prototype of the *Chûshingura* and another play called *Azuma-kagami-Mikarimaki*, which began to be acted just a month previous to the *Chûshingura*. So it will be found on examination that there is very little room left for originality, and thus the act is but a dexterous patchwork rather hastily got up for putting on the stage.

Still there are many places where the dramatic effect is felt as something unique. The first of these is the quarrel between Tonasé and O-Ishi. They are both, as wives of respectable samurai, expected to be gentle and modest, so that the passing of hot words between them is quite incongruous with their accepted character and tickles the comic sense of the audience. The comic presentation, however, of what is really tragic soon gives way to a scene of stark tragedy in which Konami waits to be slain by her mother. The pitiable sight of a beautiful girl with her hands joined meekly in prayer under an uplifted blade is sure to send a thrill through the audience. The second appearance of O-Ishi, heralded by the wedding song, is worthy of notice. Her dress is now changed to a ceremonious one with an over-garment trailing behind. And she walks with measured steps, holding a small stand according to formal custom, all quite impressive and pleasing to behold. Then her asking for the head of Honzô to be placed on the stand is something extraordinary and sounds gruesome, especially as coming from the lips of a respectable woman, reminding us of Salome asking for the head of Jokanaan. Again the sudden appearance of Honzô on the scene at the right moment, his crushing of the stand under foot, his fighting with O-Ishi, and the unexpected attack made on him by Rikiya are a succession of surprises and actions, quickly following one after another and compelling the audience to watch them with breathless interest.

Apart from dramatic presentation, this act is noteworthy as a sort of epitome of the moral ideas governing the family life of a samurai. They are, of course, old, but are by no means antiquated, and so long as the family system prevails in Japan, they are more or less approved and practised by all respectable Japanese. Marriage in Japan is more of a family affair than a personal one. It is the parents of both parties who arrange it. Not much is said

on the part of Rikiya, but we see how the parents of Konami looked for a good husband for her and finding it in
Rikiya, betrothed her to him.   And how they rejoiced at
her marriage is seen in the words of Honzô who says that
in becoming the wife of Rikiya, the worthy son of Yuranosuke unparalleled in fidelity, his daughter is a hundred
times more fortunate than if marrying into the nobility.
The wife's duty as the basis of a happy family life is well
expressed in the instructions given to her by her father.
She should, of course, cherish her husband most dearly
and also never omit to treat her parents-in-law with the
utmost respect and tenderness.   Jealousy is a vice in her
to be most carefully guarded against in any case.   So O-
Ishi never wore even an unpleasant look on meeting her
husband coming back from his debauch.   Then in case
circumstances separate man and wife, the woman, to be
virtuous, should never think of taking another husband.
So it will be seen that a Japanese woman's morality in her
wedded life is quite severe and presses almost too hard on
her side only, but nothing is unbearable when love is in
the union, as in the case of Rikiya and Konami.

The impediments to the fulfilment of the engagement
between Rikiya and Konami were two; the first was
the certainty that their marriage was destined to be only
too short-lived.   In fact the bride and bridegroom had only
one night to exchange their vows of love.   O-Ishi thought
that there could not be a more miserable mockery of joy
than to get married under such circumstances, and so rea-
sonably enough she refused to receive Konami as a bride.
But it was tided over by Konami's persistency in love
despite all trials.   The second impediment was of graver

nature.   Honzô's action in stopping Enya from wreaking his wrath on Moronao brought him into inimical relations with the retainers of Enya.   He admitted his error, but it was so serious that according to the code of samurai, it could be atoned for only with his life.   Under ordinary circumstances Honzô would have been under no obligation to do so, but in view of the alliance which he earnestly hoped would take place, he volunteered to be killed at the hand of his prospective son-in-law and so to clear the way for his beloved daughter's marriage.   The act redeemed Honzô's honour as a samurai in the eyes of Yuranosuke and his family.   Incidentally, it is to the credit of the authors that by leading Honzô to self-sacrifice, they have cleverly allayed the resentment felt by the public against his prototype Kajiwara, who stopped Lord Asano in his attempt at killing Kira.

Act X.   THE MANLINESS OF GIHEI

The scene is laid in the shop of Amagawaya-Gihei, a rich merchant at the port of Sakai.   It is now evening and he is sending out to ship several heavy boxes packed up in straw matting.   A skipper, who has come to receive the goods, goes away with them, and Gihei, left alone, observes the weather and gives a sigh of relief, thinking that it promises a fair voyage.   As he goes within, his little son Yoshimatsu comes out, led by Igo, a young apprentice, who is taking charge of the child.   They are carrying puppets and he is going to give a show with them for the child's amusement.   Igo, striking a pair of wooden clappers together, announces that it is going to commence.

They are going to play "The Crying Benkei."[1] The puppet named Yoshimatsu is to be most pitied, for he has only a father, his mother having been divorced and sent away. He cries so much for her that he is called the crying Benkei.

The child, however, gets tired of it before long and asks Igo to go and fetch his mamma.

Igo scolds him for being unreasonable and threatens to tell his master and make him send the child away too. Since last month the whole house has been turned topsy-turvy. The clerk has been discharged because he did not keep his eyes open as if he were a young mouse or something. The cook has been sent away because she gave a big yawn. And now there are only master, his little son, and himself remaining. He supposes that pretty soon they will all slip out of the house, for boxes are being sent to the ship from time to time. If they must flit, Yoshimatsu and Igo will take with them the box of puppets.

The child has now no mind for puppet-playing; he wants to sleep. So Igo says that he will sleep with him in his arms; this the child does not want, for he has no milk to give like his mamma. Igo scolds him for his unreasonableness, but really feels very sorry for the child.

At this moment two samurai appear at the door and ask for Gihei. They are Hara-Gôyemon and Ôboshi-Rikiya sent by Yuranosuke in his stead to apologize for his discourtesy in not being able to come himself, for, as the confederates are to start for Kamakura in a day or two, he is kept very busy settling this thing or that. They would like

---

1 A name given to a cry-baby.

to know if all the things ordered have been shipped all right. Gihei answers that all the weapons ordered were put in seven boxes and delivered to a skipper sailing out in the course of the evening. There remain only dark-lanterns and chain head-bands to be sent later by land.

Hara thanks Gihei for his trouble and says that though there are many merchants who received favours from Lord Enya, Gihei is the only one who possesses a spirit no less manly than a samurai's, and it is but natural that Yurano-suke should have entrusted to him this great task. But setting aside swords and spears, as coats of mail and joint-ed ladders are unusual articles, Hara wonders if any suspi-cion was aroused when Gihei bought them.

Gihei tells him that when he ordered them, he gave the makers earnest-money without telling his address and when they were made, he paid the money down and brought home so that the makers did not know who their customer was.

Rikiya then wonders how Gihei could have evaded the notice of his servants when he collected the weapons and packed them. To which Gihei replies that he took every precaution for that. When the task was entrusted to him, he sent his wife back to her father and dismissed all his ser-vants on one pretext or another, till only he, his son who is four years old, and a fool are left in the house, so that there is no danger of anyone getting wind of the plot.

Rikiya is astonished at Gihei's circumspection and prom-ises him to tell it to his father so that he may feel relieved.

The two samurai, having nothing more to ask, take their leave and go back to their inn, and Gihei is about to shut the front door, when his father-in-law, Ôta-Ryôchiku,

pushes himself in. Gihei welcomes him and asks him if
Gihei's wife, whom he sent to him for her health, is doing
well.

Ryôchiku answers that she is doing much too well. He
suspects that there is some reason for Gihei's sending her
to him for her health when there is nothing particularly
the matter with her. But be that as it may, in case the
young woman should misconduct herself while idling her
time away, her husband will be dishonoured and her
father will be compelled to cut his belly. So Ryôchiku has
a proposal to make. He would like Gihei to write a letter
of divorce to pretend to the world that he has separated
from her. Of course, when he wants her, he can take her
back at any time.

Though Ryôchiku speaks lightly, Gihei sees that he is
going to make use of such a letter. If he refuses, she will
be immediately sent back, to his great annoyance. And
though he feels that he is being caught in a trap, as he
cannot run the risk of the great undertaking being detected,
he writes the letter as desired, saying that since he gives it
to Ryôchiku, they are no longer father and son and that
there is no cause for Ryôchiku darkening his doors again.

Ryôchiku takes the letter hastily and puts it in his bosom.
He has heard, he says, that *rônin* frequented Gihei's shop
secretly. His daughter cannot tell him anything about it,
but it made him very uneasy to leave her with a son-in-
law who may do something dreadful. Fortunately he has
had a proposal of marriage from a great family and has
agreed that she should marry as soon as she gets Gihei's
letter of divorce.

Gihei is chagrined that he has thus been deliberately

entrapped, but says that even without his giving the letter
of divorce, if she has the heart to desert a husband by
whom she has a child and marry elsewhere, he has no
longing for such a woman.   She may do as she pleases.
And so saying, he seizes Ryôchiku and kicks him out.

It is now past ten o'clock and the neighbouring houses
are quite invisible in the gloom of the clouded moon.   A
patrol of several men, truncheons and cords in hand and
dark lanterns hanging at hip, make for Gihei's house.
They stop before it and one of them raps hurriedly at the
door.   To the inquiry of Gihei from within, he says that
he is the skipper who came in the evening.   There is some
error in the freight account which must be settled before
he sets asil.

Gihei fears that his loud voice will be heard by the
neighbours and so comes to the door and without any
suspicion, opens it, when he is instantly surrounded and
told that he is arrested by order.   He is greatly surprised
and asks what it all means.   But he is accused by the chief
of the patrol of being impudent to ask such a question.
As he has, at the request of Ôboshi-Yuranosuke, a retainer
of the late Enya-Hangwan, purchased weapons and equip-
ages and sent them by sea to Kamakura, he is to be seized
and tortured into confession.   He cannot escape now.

Gihei, however. denies all such things and says that they
must have hit upon the wrong man.   But the chief bids
him to hold his peace, for there is proof enough, and with
this he makes his subr 'inates bring in the long box
packed in straw matting which was stowed on board in
the evening.   On seeing it, Gihei appears greatly disturbed.   The men now set about rapidly to undo the

wrapping and are beginning to open the box, when Gihei
breaks loose suddenly and kicking them away, leaps upon
the lid to take up a firm position.

He warns them to be careful.   The box is full of various
wares and private articles ordered by the consort of a
certain daimyô.   As every one of them is marked with her
name, if the box is opened the name of this great family
will become public, and those who disclose it must take
the consequences upon themselves.

This makes the chief still more suspicious of Gihei, and
seeing that he will not readily confess, he orders one of his
men to go and fetch Gihei's little son.   As he is brought
out, the chief says that whatever the contents of the box
may be, Gihei must have joined the league of Enya's *rônin*
and be acquainted with the secrets of their plot against
Moronao's life.   Unless he confesses all, his son must pay
dearly for it.   And saying so, he points the bare blade at
the child's throat.

Gihei, however, looks on unmoved and says scornfully
that he is a man to the marrow and that even for the love
of his child, he will not confess what he does not know.

The chief expresses his astonishment at Gihei's stub-
bornness and says that he cannot take his word for it,
having furnished as he did the swords, spears, and coats of
mail, forty-six in number, all differently marked.   If he
will not make a clean breast of the whole matter, he will
be killed by inches.

It is useless, Gihei says, to frighten him with such threats.
He deals not only in weapons and armour, but also in
everything from ceremonial hats for nobles and samurai
down to straw sandals for servant lads and wenches.   If

there is anything unusual enough in that to need inquiry, every merchant in Japan will be pestered out of his life. If he is cut to death by inches, he will lose his life for his trade and does not grudge it.

And coming down from the box and thrusting his body and limbs before all, he asks them to proceed with their threats. Then snatching his little son from the grasp of the patrol, he is about to strangle him before he himself dies.

At this moment a voice is suddenly heard, calling him not to be overhasty, and from out the box comes Ôboshi-Yuranosuke, who has lain concealed in it. Filled with astonishment at this unexpected appearance, Gihei stands speechless, while the chief and the other members of the seeming patrol throw away their truncheons and cords and sit down far below their captive in a respectful attitude. Yuranosuke sits before Gihei and putting his hands on the matting, says that he hardly knows how to express his admiration for him. It is to Gihei that the phrases " the lotus rising out of the mud " and " the gold mingled in the sand " may fitly be applied. For Yuranosuke's part, he was certain of his spirit and entrusted to him the great task. But among his forty and more confederates were some who thought that since Gihei was only a merchant, he might not be trusted to keep his secret if he saw a dagger pressed at the throat of his only child. So Yuranosuke felt that the only way to put his compainons at their ease was to show them how determined Gihei's will was, and though he knew what a cruel trial it would be to Gihei, they did what was done just now. He humbly craves his pardon for their rude conduct. " Among

·flowers the cherry-blossom and among the men samurai,"
they say, but no samurai could equal Gihei in resolution.
He is thankful that he has set them such a fine example.

With these words Yuranosuke and his fellows shuffle
back and bow to Gihei three times.

Gihei shows embarrassment at their obeisance and asking them to raise their heads, says that he has done nothing
to merit the honours heaped upon him. As they say,
"Try a horse by riding and a man by associating with
him," it was natural that the gentlemen who did not know
him should feel it necessary to put him to some proof.
He was formerly a poor man but through Lord Enya's
favour, he rose to his present fortune. He was mortified
like those before him on hearing of that lord's fate, and
racked his brains to find out a means of wiping away the
great shame, but in vain. It was then that this request
came from Master Yuranosuke. Instantly he complied
with it and without troubling himself about the consequences, he did his best to execute his order. Poor, indeed, is the merchant's lot ; if he had received but a handful of rice for a stipend, he might have asked to be one of
the confiderates, following humbly in this great enterprise.
He cannot but regret his mean position. But he hopes
that when they serve their lord in the other world, they
will make mention of the little service that Gihei has done.

At these sincere words his hearers' eyes are filled with
tears. Yuranosuke then says that they are leaving for
Kamakura in the course of the night and ere long they hope
to have achieved success. He hears that Gihei has gone
so far as to send his wife away to preserve the secret and
thanks him for his great sacrifice, but he assures him that

they will enable him before long to call her home. So now he must bid him farewell.

Yuranosuke and his men prepare to depart, when Gihei stops them, saying that he should like to wish them a fortunate issue to their undertaking in a cup of *saké* before they start. Yuranosuke does not want to cause him such trouble, but hearing that Gihei has got some hand-cut buckwheat vermicelli to celebrate the occasion with, he is struck with its lucky association and remains behind with Ôwashi (Ôtaka) and Yazama to be treated to it, sending the rest of his men to join Hara and Rikiya and get as far as Sadanomori. The guests are now taken into an inner room.

At this juncture a woman comes up to the house; she is O-Sono, the wife of Gihei, who, feeling anxious for her child left behind at home, has stolen out of her father's house to have a look at her darling. She knocks at the door several times, calling for Igo. He answers from within in a sleepy tone, stumbling up out of bed. Finding the caller to be his mistress, he is glad to see her back. She tells him at the door about her misery in being banished from home, but this Igo cannot understand. She asks him about her husband; Igo cannot tell her much, only that some time ago a lot of men came, shouting 'caught, caught' as if a cat had caught a rat; and when he heard the noise, he covered his head with his quilt and went to sleep. The men are now in the house with the master, drinking *saké* and enjoying themselves. Of course, O-Sono cannot make this out but asks Igo about the child. She is told that he is asleep, not with Igo or with the master, but all alone, rolled up by himself. They tried to nurse him

to sleep, but he did not drink any milk and kept crying all
the time.   On hearing this O-Sono can bear no longer and
bursts into tears.

The voice of Gihei is heard, calling for Igo.   He comes
out and finding the boy at the door, sends him in to wait
upon the guests.   He is about to close the door, when
O-Sono holds on to it, saying that she wants so much to
speak with him.

Gihei, however, refuses point-blank and says that he
can neither listen to her nor talk with her.   She and her
father are a pair of miserable wretches ; he has nothing to
do with her.

O-Sono protests that she is not in league with her father
and has something to prove it beyond a doubt.   So saying,
she throws something folded up in through the half-opened
door at her husband's feet.

As Gihei stoops to pick it up, his wife makes her way to
his side.   He is astonished to find it to be the letter of
divorce he wrote some time since and asks her what she
means by returning it.

O-Sono reproaches him for asking her such a question.
Gihei knows well enough the evil-mindedness of her
father Ryôchiku and yet he gave the divorce-letter into his
hand.   As soon as her father brought it home, what should
he do but make preparations to have her married to another
man ?   She put a good face on the matter to throw him
off his guard and then stole the letter out of his pocket-
book and ran back home with it.   Surely Gihei loves his
child ; then how could he be so cruel as to send her away
and put the child under the care of a foster-mother ?

As O-Sono thus tearfully complains, Gihei says that the

complaint should be the other way about. When he sent her away he did not do so for any fault of hers but simply because he wished her to stay at her father's for a short time. He could not give her his reasons because her father was once a follower of Kudayû. He told her to feign illness and neglect her hair and appearance, so that she might run no risk of being troubled with offers of marriage. It is all her fault not to have heeded his instructions. As to their child Yoshimatsu, it is not she alone who is distressed about him. Though that lad Igo coaxes him from morning till evening, he calls for mamma when night falls. Gihei and the lad tell the child that mamma will be soon back and try to put him to sleep, but he will not close his eyes, and keeps on crying. Last night Gihei took up the child intending to bring him to his mother and even got so far as the door with him, but recollecting that for her to have him for one night only would be of no use at all, he only walked about, dandling and patting him till at last he fell asleep in his arms. Gihei never intended to separate her from her darling for the rest of her life, but only for a short time. And under the circumstances he could not avoid writing the divorce-letter. Her father Ryôchiku would never forgive Gihei if he were mean enough to get back the letter in this underhand manner. So he cannot receive it back. It is foreordained that the matter should stand as it is; they must be to each other for the present as if one of them had died.

As her husband ceases, O-Sono is silent for a moment. Knowing well his character, she feels that he cannot be induced to alter his determination. She has to resign herself to her fate, and thinking that perhaps this is a last parting, she asks her husband to wake up Yoshimatsu and let her have just one look at him.

Gihei, however, says that to see him for an instant and then to have to leave him would but make the pain of parting all the harder to bear. It would be well for her to go home at once. So putting the letter into her hands, he forces her out.

O-Sono cannot go away at once ; she remains at the door still entreating him at least to let her look at the sleeping face of her child. But seeing at last that there is no help for it, she turns to depart, when a couple of stout fellows, their faces muffled with only their eyes exposed, suddenly stop her. And before she can utter a cry, they seize her and, while one of them holds her fast, the other cuts her hair off at the roots and deftly possesses himself of everything she has in her bosom. The next moment, the pair run away, none can tell whither.

O-Sono has raised a cry of distress, hearing which Gihei is startled and has almost run to her assistance. But he stops at the door, gnashing his teeth and controlling himself.

At this juncture a voice calls for Gihei from within, and Yuranosuke comes out. He thanks his host for his kind hospitality and bids him farewell, as he must start before dawn. He further expresses his thanks for the great services Gihei has rendered them and turning to his companions, makes them present Gihei with a parting gift in two packages. One package is for Gihei himself and the other for his good wife O-Sono. Gihei is rather offended to have been taken as a mere merchant who has done everything for gold, but Yuranosuke assures him that the present is but a slight token of their good wishes, as they desire him to look after Lady Kaoyo after they are gone.

So saying Yuranosuke and his companions are going away from the door. Gihei, still displeased, kicks away the packages, which now, coming loose, disclose their contents. On seeing them O-Sono rushes in and is astonished to see her comb and hair-bar, her hair that was cut off, and even the divorce-letter scattered on the floor.

As Gihei stands puzzled, Yuranosuke, turning back, explains. He sent his companions Ôwashi and Yazama round by the back of the house to cut off her hair so as to make her like a nun in order to prevent her father from forcing her to marry. Before her hair grows again, he hopes that they will have attained their great object. When they have killed their enemy, Gihei and O-Sono will be reunited. Only till then O-Sono will be, as it were, a nun and Gihei may engage her as a nurse for his child. And Yuranosuke and his confederates are all sureties for her that she will divulge nothing.

Gihei now understands it all, and he and his wife thank Yuranosuke heartily. Yuranosuke replies that he deserves no thanks ; he has only repaid a small portion of the deep debt he owes Gihei. Were Gihei not a merchant, they should be overjoyed to have him with them. But as they have decided on a night-attack, when they rush into the enemy's house, they will use the name of Gihei's house, Amagawaya, as their password ; if one cries "Ama," the other shall answer "Kawa." Thus if forty and more of them call out "Ama" and "Kawa," it will be as if Gihei were with them.

With these words Yuranosuke and his companions bid

farewell again and take their departure.

Of all the episodes in the play, the one in this act is least
connected with the main plot and may well be omitted
without greatly affecting the understanding of its progress,
as is usually done in actual production along with the
bridal journey in the eighth act.   It was inserted in order to
show that even in the mercantile class a man might often
be found who had a chivalrous spirit akin to that of a
samurai.   Amagawaya-Gihei was, in fact, a fine example of
the *otokodate*, to whom reference has previously been made,
very much idealized and placed on a level higher than that
of the common run of them.

The episode was based on the story of Amanoya-Rihei,
which seems to have become current shortly after the
revenge of the Akô retainers, and which underwent subsequently many alterations and additions.   According to
the story as commonly told, Rihei was a merchant in
Osaka, whose family had for several generations enjoyed
the patronage of the Asano family.   When the loyal
retainers held council after their lord's death, Rihei went to
Akô to offer his services.   And when they had leagued
together and finally decided on a plan of revenge, Ôishi
entrusted Rihei in secret with the task of procuring all the
weapons and other things needed for the night-attack.
Unknown to his family and servants, Rihei went himself
to different shops and works to have the required things
made, and when they were ready, he forwarded them to
Yedo.   One of the smiths reported to the authorities that
he had received an order from Rihei for a special description of weapons, and Rihei was soon afterwards arrested

and examined. He eluded suspicion at the time on a certain pretext, but as other smiths, hearing of Rihei's arrest, also reported the orders received from him, he was again arrested and put to the torture, but would not disclose the truth. His wife and children were also tortured, but as they did not know, they could tell nothing. So again Rihei was subjected to such tortures as nearly killed him. He told the officers that he had from the first been prepared for death when he undertook the task, but asked them to wait for his confession till the new year; he would then submit to any punishment they might inflict upon him. He spoke with such composure that they took him at his word and waited. When the new year came, the revenge of the Akô retainers was talked about everywhere in the country, and as Rihei heard of it in prison, he confessed to the officers how his family had for several generations been patronized by the lords of Akô and how he had been asked by Ôishi to procure the weapons for the attack that he and his party made on Kira's mansion. Now that the revenge had successfully been carried out, he was ready to receive his just punishment. He added that from fear of the plot being brought to light and of the punishment he might incur being extended to innocent persons, he had concealed it even from his family. He therefore begged that his family might be spared, while he himself would willingly submit to any punishment. The officers were greatly struck with Rihei's manly spirit and went so far as to release him. His confiscated property was restored to his son to enable him to follow his father's trade. Rihei himself renounced the world and peacefully ended his days in a temple connected with the Asano family.

The story is most elaborately worked out in such a novel as the *Life of Amanoya-Rihei* by Watanabe-Katai (1865–1926). But the fictitious nature of it is proved by the fact that no one of any such name existed in the historical record relating to the Asano family. Again, in preparing for the attack, Ôishi was provided with the swords from the first as already related; spears, bows, mallets, and such things were most probably procured in Yedo for convenience, while only the firemen's mantles and hoods to be worn by all were ordered from one Wataya-Zenyemon, a former purveyor on dry-goods to the Asano family, who then lived in Kyoto. These things Ôishi carried with him in a long box as he with his attendants finally set out for Yedo.

Wataya-Zenyemon was a man not a bit behind Amanoya-Rihei in spirit. He hailed from Akô and was quite sympathetic with the loyalists, and by the letters and other documents still remaining, we know that he often gave pecuniary aids to some of them without stint. And his chivalrous spirit did not stop with them but continued even after their death, as is seen in the case of an orphan of one of the confederates, O-Hyaku by name, whom Zenyemon took under his care, seeing not only to her recovery from a long illness but also to her marriage, as if she had been his own child. So some even go so far as to think that Amanoya-Rihei might be modelled after him.

Be that as it might, the authors took the story of Amanoya-Rihei as it was already known then, and it was entirely to their credit that they wove it for the first time into the play of *Chûshingura*. The change of the name from Amanoya to Amagawaya probably occurred to them from the fact that the Portuguese sea-port of Macao in China, whence

vessels used to arrive at Sakai, was popularly known as
" Amagawa," and they adopted it for the convenience of
using it to make the sign and countersign " Ama " and
" Kawa ", which were in reality " Yama " and " Kawa".
The material was a good one, appealing as it did to the
populace, but in point of technique this act leaves much
to be desired. The use of too many petty devices is rather
tiresome and gives one an impression that the material is
not handled quite so deftly as it might have been.

Act XI. RETRIBUTION

The scene is first laid in the street before Moronao's
mansion, whose tile-roofed walls occupy the whole of the
stage. In the middle of the walls stands the massive front
gate with heavy doors to it and with a roof somewhat
higher than those of the walls. Snow lies thick on the
roofs as well as on the street. It is now long past midnight
and in the snow black figures wearing mantles and hoods
are gathering in the street. They are Ôboshi-Yuranosuke
and his men, coming now for the attainment of their long-
cherished object of taking revenge for their lord's death.
There are forty-six of them, each armed with two swords
and some other weapon. They have each his name written
in front of his mantle, besides bearing for a mark a different
letter of the Japanese alphabet for easy recognition.

As all the men assemble, Yuranosuke addresses them for
the last time, saying that as they are going to fight in the
dark, they must not forget the sign and countersign,
" Ama " and " Kawa." As has been already settled,
Hara, himself, and their company will enter by the front
gate, while Yazama, Senzaki, and their company, headed by

his son Rikiya, will press round to the rear gate. And as
soon as they are within the gates, they will rush to the attack.
They are to remember that there is but one head they have
to take.

The men have listened to their chief's command respectfully, and their spirits highly strung with a near prospect of
their success, they separate into two parties, one to attack by
the front and the other by the rear gate.

Those who remain behind set about at once to take out
a jointed ladder and bamboo poles strung like a bow from
the long box they have brought. And waiting till the
sound of the clappers of a watchman going his rounds
within the gate shall have died away in the distance, a few
of them prop the ladder up against the roof of the gate
and mounting it rapidly stand on the roof. But as the
watchman is approaching with the sound of the clappers
becoming more distinct again, they drop to the ground on
the inner side to elude his notice. But in vain, the man
sees them drop and utters an exclamation. Before he can
repeat it, however, they rush upon him, gag him, and bind
his arms tightly. " This fellow will do as a guide," they
say and opening the gate, they let all the rest waiting outside enter and close the gate again.

Here the stage revolves. The front court of the mansion
is shown with the mansion itself standing a little behind and
facing the snow-covered garden on the left. Yuranosuke
attended by Hara is seen seated on a camp stool and giving
orders. A row of shutters having been prized off, most of
the attacking party break into the house, while the rest remain outside ready for an emergency. The inmates aroused

by the uproar begin to show themselves, carrying lanterns. Women, children, and other harmless persons are allowed to escape by the rear gate, while fighting goes on here and there with the exchange of "Ama" and "Kawa" heard among the confederates. Yuranosuke shouts to his men not to look to others but aim only at Moronao. Some of Moronao's valiant retainers are hard fighters, but being surprised out of their sleep and having no time to equip themselves, they are very much at a disadvantage and fall one by one under the joint efforts of the attacking party.

Now, next door to Moronao on the north, lives Nikki-Harimanokami and on the south Ishidô-Umanojô. Both these neighbours, hearing the noise, send their men on to the walls with lanterns. They demand to know what is meant by all the uproar and confusion and the clashing of weapons. They are commanded by their lords to ascertain and report.

To this Yuranosuke replies instantly. He says that they are ex-retainers of Enya-Hangwan, forty and more in number, banded together to revenge their lord's death upon his enemy Moronao and are now struggling to get at him. They have no grudge against Lord Takauji and his brother, still less have they any quarrel with Moronao's neighbours. As they have taken every precaution against fire, no anxiety need be felt on that score. They only ask to be left alone. But if, as neighbours, the others should feel bound to assist Moronao, the attacking party are ready, despite their inclination, to turn their weapons against the intruders.

To these bold words of Yuranosuke, the retainers of the noblemen on either side of the mansion of Moronao shout back approvingly that it is but proper that those who have served a master should act as the confederates are doing. They desire the party to command their services. With these words they disappear and are heard no more.

Meanwhile the struggle with the retainers of Moronao continues, only two or three of the assailants being slightly wounded after two hours' fighting, while quite a number of the enemy are stricken down. But no one looking like Moronao is to be seen anywhere, although that light-footed Teraoka-Heiyemon has ransacked the house in search of him. He reports to the chief that he has searched every room and probed the ceilings and floors with his spear without coming upon any trace of the enemy. But as, on looking into the lord's sleeping-room, he found the bed-clothes still warm in this cold night, he thinks Moronao cannot have got far away. He will now run to see if Moronao has not escaped outside the house.

So saying he is on the point of hastening away, when he is stopped by the shrill sound of a whistle announcing that the enemy is caught. Every assailant is startled and comes towards Yazama, who now makes his appearance, dragging with him a noble-looking old man in his white silk night-dress.

Yazama reports to Yuranosuke that he found the man hidden in an outhouse, and by a faint scar on his forehead, judged him to be their enemy Moronao. But as he cannot identify him in any other way, he asks his chief's opinion on the man.

Yuranosuke is overjoyed, and feels sure that the man is Moronao ; but as even he has not met him before, he calls Senzaki, who was often sent to Moronao as a spy in the

capacity of a *hokku*-poet, to let him judge. At a glance
Senzaki gives his assurance, on which all those gathering
round give a loud shout of triumph.

Yuranosuke says that Moronao must not be put an end
to recklessly. He is at least a governor and due etiquette
must be observed in killing him. And he makes the
victim sit above himself and addressing him says that though
but humble retainers, they have ventured to force themselves within his walls, impelled by the desire of avenging
their lord's death upon him. They pray him to pardon
their want of manners and beg of him that he will now
bravely present them with his head.

On hearing these words, Moronao, though a vile sort
of creature enough, manages to keep a composed countenance and replies that he is prepared to give them his head.

Thrown off his guard for a moment, Yuranosuke approaches his prisoner, who, suddenly drawing his sword,
strikes at him, but Yuranosuke parries the blow and twists
up Moronao's arm. He derides the stroke as a clever one
and invites all his men to slake their thirst for vengeance
now. Another moment, and the body of Moronao lies
on the ground covered with wounds. The head is cut
off by Yuranosuke with the dirk that his lord left behind.

The conspirators crowding round the body are wild with
excitement; embracing each other and weeping with joy,
they exclaim, " We deserted our wives, we parted from
our children, we left our aged parents uncared for, all to
obtain this one head. What an auspicious day is this ! "

Yuranosuke takes out of his bosom his dead lord's tablet
and places it on a small table; he washes the head of its
blood-stains and offers it before the tablet; and then he

burns the incense which he has brought in his hood. He
shuffles back and bowing his head reverently three times,
nay, thrice three times to the tablet, addresses it, saying,
" O spirit of my liege lord, with awe I approach your
mighty presence. Before your sacred tablet, I set the head
of your enemy Moronao I have cut off with the dirk which
you bestowed on me in the hour of your last agony, enjoin-
ing me to give repose to your spirit. I humbly beg you
to accept my offering."

With tears he ends his speech and after a pause, invites
his comrades to burn incense one after another before the
tablet. As he is their chief commander, Yuranosuke is
asked to begin, but he declines the honour and makes
Yazama-Jûtarô take the lead because it was he to whom
fell the glory of finding Moronao and catching him alive.
Though he hesitates, as everyone is of Yuranosuke's
opinion, Yazama cannot but offer incense the first of the
company.

As Yazama finishes, Yuranosuke says that there is yet
another who should pass before him. And while everyone
is wondering who that can be, Yuranosuke draws a purse
made of striped stuff from his bosom and says that the one
who shall precede him is Hayano-Kampei. Through his
negligence of duty as a vassal, he was unable to join the
league. But eager at least to be among those who sub-
scribed for the monument to his lord, he obtained money by
selling his wife ; for that money his father-in-law was
murdered ; and the money being rejected because of his
former fault, he was mad with despair and put an end to
his life. How mortified, how desparate he must have been !
Yuranosuke has never ceased to regret having caused the

money to be returned to him. And since Yuranosuke brought Kampei to a sad end, he has never allowed the purse to leave his person and has brought it with him in the night-attack. So he asks Heiyemon to pass forward and in the name of his sister's dead husband, to burn incense before the tablet of their lord.

And Yuranosuke throws the purse to Heiyemon, who picks it up with a bow and advancing forward, offers incense in the name of Kampei. Then Yuranosuke and the rest of the company follow, burning incense in like manner and feeling truly that at last the spirit of their master is finding repose.

Suddenly a tumultuous noise of men and horses with the beating of war-drums is heard outside. Yuranosuke, however, is not in the least disturbed ; he thinks that the retainers of Moronao have returned to the attack, but as the great object of their efforts has been attained there is no need of causing any more bloodshed. So Yuranosuke is about to give the signal to his comrades to accomplish the final act of their devotion by committing *seppuku* to follow their lord to the other world, when Momonoi-Wakasanosuke rushes in. He says to Yuranosuke that Moroyasu, the young brother of Moronao, is already at the front gate. If Yuranosuke and his company commit *seppuku* at such a moment, it will be said that they were driven to it by fear and an infamous memory will attach to the deed. So Wakasanosuke counsels the party to withdraw at once to Enya's family temple, Kômyôji.

Yuranosuke thanks Wakasanosuke for his advice and begs him to guard the rear while they retire to the temple.

Hardly has Yuranosuke concluded than Yakushiji-

Jirôzayemon and Sagisaka-Bannai suddenly rush forth
from their hiding-places and, shouting that they will not
let Ôboshi escape, strike right and left at him.   Without
a moment's delay, Rikiya hastens to his father's assistance.
The struggle does not last long.   Rikiya cuts Yakushiji
down and with another stroke cuts off Sagisaka's legs so
that he falls down and soon breathes his last.   Rikiya is
praised for his prowess.   And with a tremendous shout of
triumph the scene is brought to a close.

This act is rather a short one ; it is only to bring the story
to a conclusion which is too well known to admit of any
complications.   It exists for the satisfaction of the audience
who cannot think of a play on the Akô loyalists without
a raid scene, for only there they appear in full force and as
messengers of Nemesis perform their duty.

Originally, in the first scene of this act, the landing of
Yuranosuke and his company at Kamakura by boat was
given ; but in all later versions, a scene in front of Moronao's mansion is substituted for it.   In substance both are
the same, being only the mustering of the conspirators, but
as the latter gives a view of the front gate, which is quite
impressive, it comes to be preferred to the landing scene.
And it is followed here too.

One or two points in the skilful management of the act
may be mentioned.   To the killing of Moronao, which is
the main point in issue and which alone would have suf-
ficed for the purpose of the play, the ignominious deaths of
Yakushiji, the friend of Moronao's, who figured as a
malicious commissioner in the fourth act, and Sagisaka,
that bothering follower of Moronao, are added much to the

delight of the audience.   And then the authors have not forgotten Kampei's purse, due to take part in the last act of venerating the memory of Lord Enya.   The committing of *seppuku* by the loyalists is taken here to follow as a matter of course, but it is well that the actual performance of it is deftly avoided so as not to damp the triumphal effect that has been worked up to so high a pitch.

CHAPTER VIII

APPRECIATION

It may somewhat surprise us that when we refer the *Chûshingura* to its historical sources, we find it touching them only on a few points. Indeed, what bears reference to the original facts amounts to less than a third of the whole play, the rest being all admixtures introducing novelty in order to increase the interest. Such being the case, the play, which is too long to be acted in its entirety at a single performance of a few hours, is usually cut down to half its length without any harm to the main plot.

And the main plot itself is simple enough. Even of that, the introductory part which leads to the motive force occupies one half of the whole length. The theme, which in this case is the retaliation of the wrongs done to one's master, being accepted in former days as a matter of course, needs no additional incitements to strengthen it. There exists nothing between this and its fulfilment except due preparations to ensure success for the responsible party. In history there was, indeed, something additional that retarded the action, and that was the projected restoration of the house of Asano, which was in Ôishi's mind as momentous as the idea of taking revenge and which might have overruled the latter in case his request had been granted. With this, however, the play has nothing to do, and even in regard to the preparations, it concerns itself only with a small portion of them which camouflages the leader's intention to throw the enemy off the scent. A compact sealed with blood, showing that a league has been formed, is mentioned just once in connection with Kampei's death,. but nothing is said more about the sifting out of its members and its further consolidation.   Of the privation and self- denial of the members we know only through the words of Yuranosuke, and nothing about the pathos attending them is brought on the stage.   From that the play hurries on to the last act of the night-attack, so that while it is very much simplified in that important portion which displays the noble side of loyal vengeance, much needs to be supplied from history for the proper appreciation of the story thus sketchi- ly given.

Still this has been no random result.   There is no other story of which so many attempts at dramatization have been made.   More than a hundred different plays on the subject appeared before and after the *Chûshingura* with no better success in weaving in the material.   And as attested by its popular reception, which shows no signs of decline even at the present day, the *Chûshingura* stands alone as the play of the Akô event, eclipsing all the rest and send- ing them into oblivion.

The reason is that, despite the fact that much of the im- portant material is left out of it, the *Chûshingura* is a play in which the spirit of loyalty is more elaborately depicted than in any other of the kind.   First we have the loyalty of Honzô who does all he can to avert the peril to the life and house of his master.   This soon gives way to the de- piction of more salient features of loyalty as seen in Ôbo- shi and his comrades, the features of unswerving fidelity,. unremitting tenacity of purpose, and courage in facing death.   Sincerity which dares to sacrifice everything for its vindication is also given as a mark of loyal spirit, aton-

ing for negligence of duty in the case of Kampei and in
that of the foot-soldier Heiyemon allowing him the honour
to rank with samurai and take part in the great enterprise.
Added to all this the manly spirit of the merchant, which
is but the spirit of the samurai sprouting in a different
soil, is strongly exemplified in the person of Amagawaya-
Gihei.

With this theme worked out in full, the play is well knit
in an ingenious way. Differing from the historical event,
where the Akô affair was one between the house of Asano
and Kira, in the play the two affairs, between the houses
of Momonoi and Enya and Moronao respectively, are
treated side by side by way of contrast and are connected
not only by the character of Moronao but also by the
episode connecting the families of the chief councillors of
the two houses. The story soon goes off on its proper
line, but that family affair recurs naturally towards the end,
giving occasion to an interesting dispute on marriage as
well as to the dealing of poetical justice to Honzô. Thus
in this respect the connection between the parts of the story
is well kept, conducing very much to the unity of the plot.

Family relationship, which is most naturally introduced
there, is also made a basis of connection in the group that
centres around O-Karu. She has Kampei for her husband, Heiyemon for her brother, and Yuranosuke for her
protector.

And see how often Yuranosuke appears on the stage.
Though it was otherwise in history, in the play he is made
to be in time for his master's death and have a few last
words with him, very much to the satisfaction of the spectators, who are all his admirers. From this time on, he is

in every act except some episodic ones, always acting with a dignified air and in a refined manner, even when apparently sunk in dissipation as befitting the hero which he is. This frequency of appearance is also noticed in other characters from the selected members of the league down to Sagisaka-Bannai. They are thus made familiar to the audience and help to keep the unity of the play.

We may not notice anything especially peculiar to the play in other respects, but if we compare it with the plays preceding it, we shall see that it is conspicuous by the absence of anything unnatural in the characters and incidents. Abnormal persons or persons of marvellous strength are missing here and so are supernatural interferences, and no "Deus ex machina" is resorted to. All is brought to the level of naturalness and the play is realistic from beginning to end. This is due in all probability to the fact that the material of the play was too fresh and universally known to be meddled with. At any rate it is just this quality in the *Chûshingura* that has endowed it with perpetuity as a drama, enjoyable even now with no offence to our modern rationality.

The beauty of the *Chûshingura*, however, is in part in the peculiar Japanese form in which it is written, known as *kabuki* style, as already mentioned elsewhere. Of course, this is not peculiar to the *Chûshingura* alone; indeed, all old plays were written in that style, that being the only style for plays in former days. But the charm of it has made the *Chûshingura* all the more beautiful, just as beautiful thought clad in metrical form gains so much in beauty for that very reason.

Kabuki was originally a connected series of dancing,

gesticulation and dialogue, but, with the growth of the puppet-play, was greatly influenced by it and developed to be itself on the texture of the puppet-play. The peculiarity of the puppet-play was that its text was quite poetical, to be recited by a musician to an accompaniment on the *samisen* while puppets gesticulated with suitable action. The adoption of this to *kabuki* has made it poetical and musical as well. And though recitative parts have been much reduced in consequence, still the singing of a musician and the thrumming on the *samisen* are usually heard almost all through the performance and the effect is quite operatic.

And as is suitable to such a form of composition, the words of the actors are not colloquial at all. They speak in a language which has come to be a stage one and though quite understandable, may puzzle one who hears it for the first time. The language, however, is well adapted to the peculiar intonation with which it is uttered, the intonation which is quite rhythmical and more emphatic than that of everyday speech, and is especially effective in the manipulation of cadence.

In consonance with this acting is peculiarly rhythmical and easily assumes the nature of a sort of slow dance. As it is not of a kind that could be improvised on the spur of the moment, actors have vied to establish the form most adequate to each occasion and strictly follow it, much to the delight of knowing spectators. That the acting is rhythimcal will be most clearly seen in the case of a fighting scene, in which swords and spears are brandished and crossed without lapsing into disorderly fumbling, the whole scene appearing as if regulated by an unseen mechanism, clashing and yet harmonizing as in a presto passage of orchestral music.

In this old school acting, wooden clappers beating the floor are often heard. A primitive device, to be sure, and their sharp, sudden noise may jar upon our ears, but it will be noticed that they act very much like the cymbals in an orchestral performance, accentuating some effective moment, awakening us to the consciousness of a rhythmical flow which pervades then.

Another thing in this school of acting is to be noted : that is the posturing at the end of each scene. A scene does not close with the dialogue coming to an end, but a moment is always reserved after that for the actors to remain in significant posturing expressive of the sentiment of the occasion, a tableau vivant which goes far to help us retain the impression made by the acting.

Thus the whole thing in the old drama *kabuki*, the text and its acting with constant accompaniment of music, is rhythmical and forms an artistic world of its own ; and one who enjoys it comes first of all to steep himself in its atmosphere which poetizes any story done up in this style.

So it will be seen that the old style of the *Chûshingura* is really its strong point and helps to make it, in conjunction with other excellent qualities, unsurpassed by any attempt, if such be ever tried, at modernization. It is very fine as it is and should be recommended to the appreciation of all who love poetry and art.

INDEX

A

Akô, whereabouts of, 19; news of Asano's tragedy reaching, 20.

Akô Castle, arrangement for surrendering, 33-4; formal delivery of, 38.

Amagawaya-Gihei, 114, 200f, 213; arrested and examined by a seeming patrol at his house, 204-6; opening his heart to Yuranosuke and his fellows, 207.

Amanoya-Rihei, 213-6.

Ancester-worship, the Japanese, 97-100.

Araki, Government officer to take delivery of Akô Castle, 31, 37, 38; writing a letter to Ôishi, 46.

Artisans, 110,

Asano, Lady; visited by Ôishi, 48-50.

Asano-Daigaku, See Daigaku.

Asano-Takuminokami, Lord of Akô, 1, 3; appointed as official entertainer, 9; maliciously treated by Kira, 11-3; attacking Kira, 13; in custody of Lord Tamura, 15; ordered to commit *seppuku*, 15; dying letter of, 16; scene of *seppuku* of, 17-8; dying ode of, 18; delivery of the mansion of, at Teppôzu, 18-9.

Ashikaga-Tadayoshi, 115f, 123.

B

Bannai, retainer of Lord Enya, 124f; coming out to seize Kampei, 130; coming with Ono-Kudayû to watch Yuranosuke, 163-4; coming out with Yakushiji to attack Yuranosuke and killed by Rikiya, 223.

C

Chikamatsu-Monzayemon, the Shakespeare of Japan, 3, 4.

Chikara, Ôishi's son, called before his father, 60-1; to lead one company in making a raid on Kira's mansion, 70.

Chisaka, councillor of Lord Uesugi, 44-5; aiding Kira, 58.

Chûshingura, the, an old Japanese play and why famous, 1; The gist of the story of, 1; written when and by whom, 2; the occasion of writing, 4; how long and how to be enjoyed, 5, 6-8; appreciation of, 225f.

Chûshingura, the meaning of, 2.

Class distinctions, 110.

Common people, 108f.

Conference, at Akô Castle, the first, 20f; the second, 26-31; the third, 32-3; the fourth, 34-6; at Maruyama, 63-4.

Confucius, on vengeance, 92.

D

Daigaku, Asano's brother, suggested to inherit the house, 21; Ôishi petitioning on behalf of, 39; relegated, 63.

Daimyô, feudal lords, 9.

Date-Sakyônosuke, Lord of Yoshida, appointed as official entertainer, 9, 10.

Delegates of Akô retainers, at Yedo, 31; return of, 32.

E

Enya-Hangwan, 1, 4, 106f, 126; handing to Moronao a letter-box from his wife, 129; attacking Moronao for being insulted, 129; committing *seppuku*, 137.

F

Family, a Japanese, importance of per-

petuating, 100-1.
Farmers, 108-9.
Filial piety, versus loyalty, 87-8 ; due also to ancestors, 100.

G

Goban-Taiheiki, the, a play by Chikamatsu, 3.

H

Hanamichi, 'flowery way', 119.
Hara-Gôyemon, chief retainer of Enya, coming to inquire after his lord's health, 134; visiting Kampei with Senzaki, 157f; visiting Amagawaya-Gihei with Rikiya, 201-2.
Hara-Sôyemon, reporting the Yedo affairs, 20; having a private talk with Ôishi, 22-3 ; cowing Ôno, 25 ; sent by Ôishi to pacify confederates, 47; the opinion of, at Yamashina conference, 55-6 ; at the raid, 75-7.
Hatamoto-yakko, 113.
Hayano-Kampei, *See* Kampei.
Hearn, Lafcadio, view of, on the Japanese vendetta, 96.
Heiyemon, coming to see his chief, 164f ; permitted to accompany his chief to the East, 176.
Honzô, councillor of Wakasanosuke, 120f; offering presents to Moronao, 125-6; stopping Enya from killing Moronao, 129; appearing at Yuranosuke's and offering his own head as a bridal gift, 191 ; wounded by Rikiya, 193 ; confessing his real intention to Yuranosuke, 193-4; offering a plan of Moronao's mansion to Rikiya, 195.
Hori, 140.
Horibe-Yasubyôye, pressing Ôishi to speedy action, 46-7.

I

Ichimonjiya, master of a tea-house in Gion-machi, 152f.

Ichiriki, Ichimonjiya's tea-house, 163.
Isogai-Jûrôzayemon, Asano's retainer, 16, 26.
Ishidô-Umanojô, Commissioner, 136.
Iyeyasu, "Legacy" of, quoted, 84; injunction of, on vengeance, 92.

K

Kabuki, term for old Japanese plays, 5 ; how developed 228-9; charm of, 229-30.
Kajiwara-Yosôbei, 13, 132.
Kakogawa-Honzô, *See* Honzô.
Kampei, retainer of Enya, 126; making love with O-Karu in a pine-grove, 127 ; hurrying back and feeling uneasy on Enya's account, 129 ; trying to kill himself for his disloyalty, 130; advised by O-Karu to go to her home, 130; living as a hunter, 143 ; meeting Senzaki and promising to subscribe to the erection of a monument for Enya, 144-6 ; killing accidentally a man and making off with his pouch, 149 ; coming home, 153 ; erronously concluding that he killed his own father-in-law, 155 ; visited by Hara and Senzaki, 157f ; being overhasty in committing suicide, 158; admitted into the league, 159; why committing suicide, 161 ; made second to offer incense before his lord's tablet, 221-2.
Kanadehon-Chûshingura, the full title of the *Chûshingura*, 2.
Kanzaki-Yogorô, showing detective skill, 69.
Kaoyo, Lady, wife of Lord Enya, 10f; arranging flowers, 134.
Katakiuchi, vengeance, 91 ; the motto for, 92; moral qualities attendant on, 94-6.
Kataoka-Gengoyemon, Asano's headpage, 16; the last meeting of, with his lord, 17, 26.
Kayano-Sampei, 132-3.

Kegakuji, the family temple of Asano at Akô, 41.

Kenkôhôshi-Monomiguruma, the, a play by Chikamatsu, 3.

Kira-Kôzukenosuke, 3 ; Grand Master of Ceremonies, 9, 10; malicious towards Asano, 11-3 ; wounded by Asano, 14; on guard, 44 ; effect on, of Ôishi's staying in Yedo, 52; supported by Lord Uesugi, 58 ; killed at last, 77.

Kiyomori, 88.

Konami, daughter of Honzô, betrothed to Rikiya, 121-1; taking a long journey with her mother to Yamashina, 182f; asking her mother to prevent her marriage from being broken, 188 ; beseeching her mother to take her life, 189.

Kôno-Moronao. *See* Moronao.

Kudayû, coming to inquire after his lord's health, 134; opinion of, on the disposal of Enya's mansion, 138-9; coming to watch Yuranosuke at Ichiriki, 163-4; trying to fathom Yuranosuke's mind, 169-70; concealing himself under the verandah, 171 ; reading Yuranosuke's letter by moonlight, 172 stabbed by Yuranosuke, 177-8.

Kugé, Court nobles, 107.

L

League, loyal, formed, 28-30; number of members of 64-5, 68.

" Legacy " of Iyeyasu, 84.

Loyalists, forty-seven, ages of, 72; attire of, 73 ; raid made by, on Kira's mansion, 75f; reporting their deed before Asano's grave, 78-9; in custody of four lords, 80; condemned to commit *seppuku*, 81; where buried, 81.

M

Marriage in Japan, 198-9.

Merchants, 110.

Michiyuki, progress scene, explained, 182.

Mimura-Jirôzayemon, servant at Akô Castle, 29-30.

Mitford, *Tales of Old Japan* by, referred, 82, 145.

Momonoi-Wakasanosuke. *See* Wakasanosuke.

Moronao, 4, 115f; making unlawful suit to Kaoyo, 117 ; at the gate of Tadayoshi's palace, 124; bribed by Honzô, 125-6; insulting Enya and wounded by him, 129 ; caught at last by his enemy, 219 ; beheaded by Yuranosuke, 220.

N

Nakamura-Ganjirô, actor, 3.

O

Ôboshi-Yuranosuke. *See* Yuranosuke.

Ôdera, 140.

O-Ishi, Yuranosuke's wife, 184; refusing to have Konami for her son's wife, 186f; consenting to her son's marriage, 190; asking for Honzô's head as a bridal gift, 191 ; telling her reason for having objected to the marriage, 195.

Ôishi-Kuranosuke, 4; summoning Akô retainers to an extraordinary meeting, 20; having a private talk with Yoshida and Hara, 22-3 ; opinion of, on samurai's part, 24; unbosoming himself to the confederates, 30; handing a petition to Government officers, 39-40; last night of, at Akô Castle, 40-1; at Yamashina, 43-4; making use of Reikôin temple, 45 ; letter to, from Araki, 46; visiting Yedo, 48 ; holding a general meeting in Yedo, 50-1; holding meetings at Yamashina, 53-7; debauchery of, 58-60, 62; sounding his son Chikara's mind, 60-1; divorcing his wife, 61–2; ordering upper garments for confederates, 64; starting for Yedo for good, 65; at his hotel in Yedo, 67f; detailed instructions of, 68; paying farewell homage to Asano's grave, 70; final instructions of, 70–1; holding a religious rite before Asano's tomb to report the consummation of vengeance 78–9; motto of, 87; firm hold of, on the Japanese ethical basis, 102.

Okajima-Yasoyemon, treasure of the Akô Clan, 36; enraged with Ôno, 36–7.

O-Karu, mistress of Ôishi, 62.

O-Karu (in the play), maid of Kaoyo and sweetheart of Kampei, 126f; at her home in the country 151f; carried away by Ichimonjiya, 155; character of, 160–1; reading Yuranosuke's letter by its reflection on her mirror, 172; arousing Yuranosuke's suspicion, 172; going to be redeemed by Yuranosuke, 173–4; met by her brother Heiyemon, 174; told why she must die, 174–6; forgiven by Yuranosuke, 176.

O-Kaya, O-Karu's mother, 151f.

Ôno, suggesting to appeal for the continuance of Asano's house, 21; decamped, 37.

Ono-Kudayû. See Kudayû.

O-Sono, Gihei's wife, 208f.

Ôtaka-Gengo, 65; finding out when Kira would be at home, 69–70.

Ôta-Ryôchiku, Gihei's father-in-law, 203–4.

Otokodate, 113–4.

Ôtomo-no-Yakamochi, quoted, 90.

P

Passwords, in history, 71; in the play, 212.

Pledge of the league, signed, 28–9; renewed, 57; renewed again, 68.

R

Reikôin, temple in Kyoto, 45.

Restoration of Asano's house, Ôno suggesting to appeal for, 21; Yoshida thinking it first duty to work for, 22; Ôishi's appeal for, 39; why important, 99–101; what would follow if granted, 101–2; spirit shown by Ôishi concerning, 104.

Rikiya, Yuranosuke's son, as messenger from his master Enya to Wakasanosuke, 120; at his mistress's side, 134; coming to see his father at Ichiriki with a letter from Lady Kaoyo, 163; stabbing Honzô, 189; killing Yakushiji and Bannai, 223.

Ruskin, quoted, 87.

S

Sadakurô, Kudayû's son, 139; robbing and killing Yoichibei, 147–9; killed by a stray shot, 149.

Sagisaka-Bannai. See Bannai.

Sakakibara, Government officer to take delivery of Akô Castle, 31, 37, 38.

Sampei. See Kayano-Sampei.

Samurai, motto of, 22, 83; primary duty of, 86; limitations of the spirit of the, 88–9; rise of the spirit of the, 89; fusion of the spirit of the, with Yamato-Damashii, 91; veracity of, 95–6; a true, 102; civil duties of, 103–4; combining the military and ruling classes, 107–8.

Sawamura-Sôjûrô, actor, 4.

Seal of blood, significance of, 95.

Self-sacrifice, the custom of, 83–5.

Sengakuji Temple, Ôishi visiting his lord's grave at, 48; the party's farewell homage to Asano's grave at, 70; a Mecca of admirers of loyal spirit 81.

Senzaki-Yagorô, differing in opinion from Kudayû, 139; meeting Kampei accidentally, 144–6; visiting Kampei with Hara, 157–60; coming to sound his chief at Ichiriki, 164f.

Seppuku, disembowelment, 14, 15, 17–8; con-comittant punishments to, 18; appearing first in Japanese history, 105; adopted as a form of capital punishment, 105; selection of the abdomen for, 105–6; fitness of, in self-dispatch, 107.

Shigemori, 88.

Spies, sent by Chisaka, 45.

T

Taiheiki, the, a historical story-book, 3, 4.

Takauji, Shogun, first of the Ashikaga line, 3.

Takemori-Tadashichi, coming to sound his chief at Ichiriki, 164f.

Tamura-Sakyôdayû, Lord of Ichino-seki, 15.

Tennyson, quoted, 86.

Teraoka-Heiyemon. *See* Heiyemom.

Terasaka-Kichiyemon, sent by Ôishi to report to Lady Asano, 79–80.

Theatres in the Tokugawa period, 5.

Tokugawa Government, 2.

Tonasé, wife of Honzô, 120; coming to visit Yuranosuke with her daughter Konami, 185f; altercating with O-Ishi in marrying Konami to Rikiya, 186f; trying to kill herself, 189.

Tsunayoshi, Shogun, in anger with Asano, 14; hesitating to make up his mind in passing judgment on the loyalists, 81.

Tsurugaoka Hachiman, 115.

U

Uesugi, Lord of Yonezawa, 44.

V

Vendetta, the Akô, the gist of the story of, 1; not one of ordinary vengeance, 97; of Soga brothers 2; the Japanese, religious significance of, 96; cases of, in the Tokugawa period, 110–1.

Vengeance. *See Katakiuchi*.

W

Wakasanosuke, 106f; telling Honzô his intention of killing Moronao, 121; dumbfounded at the change of Moronao's attitude towards him, 128; coming to advise Yuranosuke's party to withdraw at once to Enya's family temple, 222.

Wataya-Zenyemon, 215.

Y

Yakushiji-Jirôzayemon, Commissioner, 136, 138–40; coming to attack Yuranosuke and killed by Rikiya, 223.

Yamagishi-Kunai, 4.

Yamashina, Ôishi's retirement at, 43.

Yamato-Damashii, spirit of Japan, 90–1.

Yatô-Yemonshichi, boy-page of Asano, 28–9.

Yazama-Jûtaro, 140; coming to sound his chief at Ichiriki, 164f; catching Moronao alive at an outhouse 219.

Yoichibei, robbed and killed by Sada-kurô, 147–9; carried home on a shutter, 156.

Yonezawa Clan, 44.

Yoshida-Chûzayemon, 22, 23; hastening to Yedo with the resolution passed at Yamashina, 57.

Yuranosuke, 4; at his master's last hour, 137–8; given Enya's dirk, 138; holding consultations with retainers, 138–9; telling his intentions to his confederates, 140; at his revels, 163f; eating offered fish on the eve of the anuniversary of his lord's death, 170; leaving his rusted sword behind, 171; reading Kaoyo's letter, 172; stabbing Kudayû through the floor, 177; ordering Heiyemon to take Kudayû to the

River Kamo, 178 ; character of, how delineated, 181 ; rolling the snow up into a big ball, 184 ; going to Sakai as an itenerant minstrel, 197 ; appearing out of a box at Gihei's and expressing admiration for him, 206 ; doing something for Gihei's wife, 212 ; coming to attack Moronao, 216f ; cutting Moronao's head off, 220 ; offering Moronao's head before the tablet of his lord, 220-1.